LEADERSHIP
IMPACT

Published by Patience Publishing House
First edition, 2025

Copyright © 2025 by Aaron Patience
All rights reserved. No part of this book may be reproduced, stored in a retrieval system, or transmitted in any form or by any means—electronic, mechanical, photocopying, recording, or otherwise—without the prior written permission of the publisher or author.

Patience Publishing House™
Miami, Florida
www.aaronpatience.com

ISBN (Hardcover): 979-8-9988-137-0-2
ISBN (Paperback): 979-8-9988137-8-8
ISBN (eBook): 979-8-9988137-2-6

Cover Design by Damonza Studio
Interior Design by Vanessa Mendozzi
Copyediting by Hugh Barker
Proofreading by Kelly Lydick
Website Design by Aaron Patience

DEDICATION

To my incredible wife, Vanessa, whose love, support, and friendship over the years have meant everything.

To our three wonderful children, Jake, Dylan, and Abby — you bring joy into our lives and remind me every day what truly matters most.

LEADERSHIP
IMPACT

HOW LEADERS DEVELOP OTHERS
AND CREATE TRUE IMPACT

AARON PATIENCE

Contents

1.	Flexible, Fluid, and Ready to Pivot	1
2.	The Push	5
3.	Clearing the Desk	7
4.	Knowing When to Merge	11
5.	Intentionality in Warmth	13
6.	Vested	15
7.	Built for Action or Inaction	17
8.	Elbows Out	19
9.	The Power of Presence	21
10.	Order Up!	23
11.	I Fix Appliances	27
12.	Labels: Temporary or Transformative	29
13.	Finding My Voice	31
14.	Who's Right?	33
15.	A Test of Limits, a Path to Growth	37
16.	Leadership, Doubt, and Owning Your Space	41
17.	Two Steps at a Time	45
18.	The Effort Behind Mastery	47
19.	I Heard You, I Just Wasn't Listening	51
20.	The Power of the Peloton	53
21.	On the Side of the Road	55
22.	Powerful Moments	57
23.	The Shopping Cart	59
24.	Quiet Courage	61

25.	Something Just Fell	63
26.	Locked Out, but Not for Long	67
27.	A Soldier's Manual	69
28.	Preparation and Trust	73
29.	When the Wave Hit	77
30.	A Leader, a Lesson, a Lasting Moment	81
31.	A Lesson in Success	85
32.	One Word	87
33.	The Joy in Every Horrible Shot	89
34.	Humor, Care, and the Middle Seat	91
35.	Keeping Your Eyes Up	93
36.	The Illusion Of Leadership	95
37.	Trusting the Process, Trusting the Person	97
38.	The Power of Being Seen	99
39.	I Am Not Alone	101
40.	A Lesson in Expertise	103
41.	Right Conditions	105
42.	Every Drop Matters	107
43.	Wider Views Await	109
44.	The Room Was Watching	113
45.	The Guidance Gap	117
46.	Humble to a Fault	121
47.	Questions You're Not Supposed to Ask	125
48.	Delray Beach	129
49.	Encore	133
50.	Owning the Feedback	135

About the Author	139
Acknowledgments	141

About the Cover

The compass rose on the cover drew me in from the beginning. There's something about it that feels timeless and directional, without being rigid. Early on, I made the decision to omit the traditional cardinal points. That choice was intentional. Leadership doesn't follow one direction. It shifts depending on where someone is and what they're navigating next.

The needle introduces a quiet touch of color, but it's more than design. It's a nod to the idea of a moral compass. For me, that includes honesty, respect, compassion, care, and the ability to discern what's right. I may never call those values out directly—but they're in here. Threaded throughout.

The title, *Leadership Impact,* felt right. I considered other variations, but kept coming back to the idea that real impact is defined by how others experience your leadership. It's not about being loud. It's about being lasting.

Before You Begin

Leadership Impact brings together a series of real stories, drawn from 30 years of leadership, shaped by both success and challenge. These are my lived experiences, offered with clarity and intent. Each one delivers a practical perspective, something to apply, consider, or carry forward.

This isn't theory. This is leadership as it happens, in the moments that shape us.

This is Leadership Impact. Enjoy the journey.

Let who you are,
not just what you do,
leave the lasting impression.

AARON PATIENCE

CHAPTER 1

Flexible, Fluid, and Ready to Pivot

What makes adaptability one of the most important tools we have?

A simple rule of thumb can often guide us through even the most complex challenges. Over the years, lessons from leaders, unexpected turns in life, and moments of discomfort have shaped the way I think about change. Some ideas stay with us, not because they are flashy or complex, but because they hold up. They work in practice. They get you through.

For me, one of those is a phrase I have carried for many years. I have said it in meetings, in coaching sessions, in casual conversations, and in quiet moments by myself.

Be flexible, fluid, and ready to pivot.

At first, it sounds like something you would see on a whiteboard. But like all good things, its strength is in the substance behind the words. This mindset has served me in rooms filled with uncertainty, in conversations filled with emotion, and in seasons of work that did not go the way anyone expected.

Here is what it means to me.

Flexible

Being flexible is not about giving in. It is about holding your shape under pressure without breaking. It is about understanding that the original plan is not always the final plan. Flexibility means you can adjust with intention in a mindful way. You are not stuck. You are aware. You can move when the moment calls for it. Some of the most effective leaders I have known did not lose their values when things changed. But they did know how to bend their approach to meet the moment.

Fluid

To be fluid is to stay in motion: not in a hurry, not frantically, but moving. It is the idea that progress does not have to look like a straight line. It is the ability to respond to what is around you and still make headway. Fluidity brings grace to the way we lead. It allows us to let go of the idea of perfect conditions and find our rhythm in real ones. I think of it as being responsive without being reactive. There is strength in that distinction.

Ready to Pivot

This is not about scrambling. It is about preparation. Being ready to pivot means you are aware of your surroundings. You are not just reacting to change, you are positioned for it. You are looking ahead. You have built enough clarity and calm into your process that, when the turn comes, you can make it without panic. Pivoting well is a skill. It takes practice, self-awareness, and often a good dose of courage. But once you learn this skill, it becomes part of how you operate.

Together, these three qualities make up something deeper

than a saying. They reflect a way of being—a way of thinking. They are a reminder that adaptability is not about being passive or overly agreeable. It is not about always saying yes, but nor it is about never holding firm. True adaptability requires effort. It means that you stay present. You think clearly. And when necessary, you put your shoulder into the work and move it forward.

Even the simplest tools must be revisited. If they are going to stay sharp, they need your ongoing attention. The mindset I am describing is no different. It helps you to pause and ask yourself how you are showing up. Are you holding too tightly to the way things were supposed to go? Are you fluid enough to adjust your pace, without losing direction? Are you paying attention, so that when the time comes, you are ready to pivot?

In leadership and in life, the ones who adapt are often the ones who continue. The ones who grow. The ones who build trust. Not because they always knew what would happen, but because they stayed ready for anything that might happen.

It is simple. It is practical. And it holds up.

Be flexible. Be fluid. Be ready to pivot.

This phrase has become a cornerstone of my leadership message over the years. It has helped guide teams, shape decisions, and, in many ways, hold things together when everything felt uncertain. It is also, if I am being honest, one of the phrases that has helped me keep my sanity. That last part may be said with a smile, but the truth behind it runs deep.

In times of pressure, complexity, and unexpected change, this mindset has offered both clarity and calm. And I suspect I am not the only one who needs both.

CHAPTER 2

The Push

In cycling, "the push" is an unspoken code. A hand placed firmly on the shoulder by another rider, not in dominance, but in solidarity. It's the silent support during a steep climb, a battle against a headwind, or a quiet crisis in the middle of the ride. No announcement. No fuss. Just the push.

I was deep into a long ride, somewhere between exhaustion and doubt, with my feet off the pedals and my spirits low. The road stretched out, quiet and punishing. I had pulled over, with my head bowed, questioning whether I could finish.

Out of nowhere, another cyclist pulled up beside me. He stopped, scanned me briefly, and asked with a calm authority, "Are you injured or hurt?" "No," I replied, a bit startled. "Good. Get on the bike and let's go."

That was it. No motivational speech. No time wasted. He saw something in me, and knew that, in that moment, I couldn't summon the ability to keep going. His certainty became my ignition. I clipped back in, pushed off, and just like that, I was riding again.

Months later, on a different ride, I found myself with a close friend who had sustained an injury many miles into a long route. This time, I was the one assessing to situation. Without a word, I placed my hand on his shoulder. A firm, steady touch to keep him upright and moving. No words were exchanged. We both understood the gesture.

That's leadership.

Not always planned. Rarely perfect. Often silent.

It's the decision to act when someone else is faltering. To offer your strength without waiting for permission. To carry someone just a bit when they can't quite carry themselves.

Some of the most powerful leadership moments are like that—quiet, instinctive, and human.

To those who've given me that push, in work, in life, or in leadership, thank you. You may not even know the full weight of what you did.

If this story brings someone to mind, maybe now's the time. Reach out. Offer the push. Or simply say thank you to the one who offered it to you.

CHAPTER 3

Clearing the Desk

The team and I had just come through our second or third merger in a span of a few years. Layered on top of that were major shifts in leadership duties and internal expectations. It was a lot to deal with. Weeks turned into months, and despite our best efforts, we were still dragging around old habits, doing what we had always done, even though our future demanded something different.

I tried everything—conversations, coaching, and redirection. I offered context, explained the why, shared the strategy. But it wasn't landing.

We were never going to get to the new work—the real work—if we kept doing things the old way.

So I decided to show them.

At our next leadership meeting, I packed the room. We were shoulder to shoulder, nearly hitting the fire code limit. At the front of the room, I cleared a space for a single small table.

On that table, I piled everything you might find on a professional's desk: coffee mugs, water bottles, a phone, pens, highlighters, paper clips, notebooks, a stapler, a hole punch, folders, chargers, a monitor, keyboard, and even a desk lamp. It was all there: an exaggerated version of our day-to-day environment.

I sat at the table and asked the room to focus. I explained that everything on the table represented things I had once thought I needed to get the job done. But over time, I had realized many of those items were simply… fixtures. They'd been there so long, they had become part of the scenery. Whether they were useful or not didn't matter. They stayed because they'd always been there.

I told the team that each object symbolized something in our work routines: old habits, outdated tasks, or default behaviors that no longer served us but still occupied our time.

Then I paused.

And I said, "It's our duty to clear the desk. We have to let go of what no longer moves us forward."

I reminded them of something our CEO had once said: "We need to tear it down so we can build it back up, brick by brick."

And with that, I swept the entire contents of the table off with both arms.

Papers flew. The phone hit the ground. A wave of water splashed into the front row. Some teammates jumped up to clean the mess, instinctively trying to restore order.

I held my hand up, to let them know they should leave it. The room fell silent.

There was no anger. No scolding. This wasn't about theatrics or frustration. It was a moment of clarity, designed with care. I needed them to see the clutter to feel the weight of what we were still holding onto, even when it no longer helped us grow.

Clearing the Desk

We sat in that silence for a while. The mess stayed on the floor, untouched. And then, slowly, I turned their attention to what remained.

The table. It was clear. Open. Ready.

That was our real estate. That was our calendar. That was our capacity. We finally had room to choose what to add back in—what truly mattered, one item, one action, and one intentional step at a time.

Yes, I may have been guilty of a little dramatic flair. But it worked.

Not because I made a mess, but because I made a point.

Sometimes the most productive thing a leader can do is clear the desk, not out of anger, but out of clarity. Not to discard the past, but to make space for the future we're ready to build.

CHAPTER 4

Knowing When to Merge

A few years ago, I was driving my then leader through South Florida traffic after a client meeting. I did what I had always been taught: stay in line, wait patiently, and follow the rules. About a half-mile from our exit, I was already in the proper lane, holding my place as cars sped past in the adjacent lane, all of them planning to cut in near the front. It always frustrated me, but I stayed put, certain I was doing the right thing.

My leader glanced over and said, "Aaron, this is the same reason you may not find certain kinds of success. I never get in line this early. I go to the end and merge in. That's how the flow works."

To me, it felt off. Maybe even a bit rude. I believed in taking your turn. But what I've come to realize over time is that going to the front isn't always about entitlement. Sometimes it's about understanding that the option is available to you, too. And that using it with thoughtfulness and timing is not wrong. It's simply a choice.

It's not about cutting corners. It's about navigating real-world situations with awareness, not just adherence. Knowing the rules matters. However, so does knowing how to move within them when others aren't following the same playbook.

When I taught my son to drive, I focused on the rules, every one of them. But over time I've made sure he understands something more. Awareness is a skill. Adapting doesn't mean abandoning principles. It means applying them with wisdom. Reading traffic. Reading people. Adjusting as needed with intention.

Lining up early reflects something good: patience, order, and fairness. I believe in that. But leadership sometimes asks you to see more—to know that others won't always play by the same rules, and to choose how you respond with clarity, not just frustration.

Of course, this isn't a story about traffic.

It's a story about perspective, and the quiet moments that stretch your understanding of how and why other people move. Leadership is often about more than taking your place. It is about seeing the landscape, anticipating change, and making decisions that balance values with velocity.

You may still see it differently. I once did, too. But if we refuse to understand how others are moving through the world, we may find ourselves stuck, holding our place, while others continue to move forward.

Sometimes success is knowing when to stay in line.

Other times it is knowing when to merge.

CHAPTER 5

Intentionality in Warmth

Walk into any hospital and you will notice something quiet but powerful happening behind the scenes. A nurse walks by, offers a kind smile, and without needing to be asked, hands a patient a warm blanket. It is not dramatic. It is not loud. But it is intentional.

Hospitals provide warm blankets, not just as a necessity, but as an act of care. In a place that is often cold, unfamiliar, and filled with uncertainty, warmth becomes more than physical. It becomes a gesture of comfort, reassurance, and humanity. That simple offering says, "You matter. You are not alone. I see you."

There is something about that moment. The timing, the delivery, and the understanding. It stays with people. Not because it solved the problem or answered every question, but because it acknowledged something real. It met a need before it had to be spoken aloud.

As leaders, we are given the same opportunity every day. Our version of a warm blanket might not be literal, but the principle is the same. Do we notice when someone on our team is off?

Do we check in with real curiosity, or offer encouragement when it is least expected but most needed?

Leadership is not just about strategy, performance, and direction. It is also about attentiveness. It is about choosing to slow down enough to see the people behind the work and making deliberate choices to demonstrate care. When we are intentional in the way we lead, people feel it. When we are warm in the way we show up, it leaves a mark.

A quick message to acknowledge someone's effort; a well-timed question that signals we are paying attention; a moment of support during a difficult period: These small acts matter. They speak volumes about who we are and what we value.

The impact of intentional care is not fleeting. It builds trust. It deepens connection. It creates a space in which others feel seen, safe, and supported. That is not just a nice idea. It is a leadership advantage. Teams that feel cared for are more engaged, more resilient, and more willing to stretch themselves, because they know they are not doing it alone.

I often think about the legacy we leave as leaders—not the accolades or the outcomes, but how people remember what it felt like to work with us. Were we present? Were we kind? Did we create warmth in cold places?

Just like the nurse who offers the blanket before the words are even spoken, we have a chance to meet the moment before it becomes a crisis. We can lead with calm, offer reassurance, and choose care. Not once, but consistently.

Intentional warmth is not soft. It is strong. It is steady. And it makes a difference.

May we all strive to lead with that same warmth in mind.

CHAPTER 6

Vested

Should people be vested in their work? Yes, of course. But to what degree? That question matters more than most people realize.

Being invested in your work, your team, your clients, and your outcomes is what gives meaning to what you do. When you care deeply about the mission and the people around you, you lead with intention. You build trust. You build momentum. You build something that feels like it matters.

But there is a fine line between being vested and being consumed.

We often celebrate deep commitment. We admire the leaders who go the extra mile, who give their time, energy, and focus without hesitation. But being overly invested in one area, whether it is the company, the team, the cause, or the goal, can come at a cost. It can begin to shift from purpose to pressure, and from contribution to personal cost.

Without balance, being fully vested may quietly erode your sense of self. It can blur boundaries. It can drain your energy. And over time, it can impact your health and your relationships. What begins as service can turn into sacrifice, and not always the kind that leads to something greater.

This is not a call to care less. It is a call to notice when caring starts to cost you more than it should.

The healthiest leaders I have known are not the ones who hold back. They are the ones who stay self-aware. They have clarity about where their energy is going and why. They know how to realign when something feels off. They recognize when a part of their commitment is out of rhythm with the rest of their life.

It helps to pause and ask: What am I truly vested in right now? Is it aligned with my values, or just with the expectations around me? Am I connected to the purpose of the work, or simply caught up in the momentum of it?

Being vested is powerful when it is tied to values, not just effort. When you invest in something that aligns with who you are and what you believe in, the energy it returns is sustaining.

However, when your identity is tied too closely to outcomes, titles, or external validation, even success can leave you feeling empty.

Awareness is the first shift. It allows you to step back and see the full picture. It gives you the space to reset, to reinvest with intention, and to build a kind of presence that is both strong and sustainable.

We are meant to care. That is not the issue. The question is whether the way we are investing ourselves still reflects who we are, or whether it has started to cost us something we did not mean to give away.

Purpose is not found in pouring everything out. It is found in knowing what you are pouring yourself into, and why.

CHAPTER 7

Built for Action or Inaction

Like many people, I have trained myself to respond immediately to alarms. When it rings, I move. One single tone is all it takes. There is no back-up, and no second chance. It is a habit that signals clarity—a moment that triggers immediate action.

But reminders? That is a different story.

Reminders carry a different kind of permission. They can be pushed forward. Delayed. Snoozed. Ignored. And the more that happens, the easier it becomes to detach yourself from the original intent. It is not that the task is unimportant. It is that repetition without urgency slowly chips away at priority.

What I have realized is this: We often build habits without realizing it. Every time I act immediately on an alarm, I reinforce readiness. Every time I delay a reminder, I reinforce avoidance. Over time, those patterns shape more than just the way I start my day. They shape the way I move through work, decision-making, and leadership.

There is value in knowing the difference.

Some things are built for immediate response. They are alarms that, when they call, should be answered without delay.

They carry urgency, direction, and a call to act.

Other things allow for flexibility. They are reminders—signals that matter but do not demand immediate movement. They still count. But they also allow space to reflect, reprioritize, or revisit.

Neither approach is wrong. The key is recognizing the difference and being honest about which you are dealing with. Are you responding to an alarm with the discipline it requires? Or are you treating it like a reminder and losing momentum? Are you giving yourself permission to pause when needed, or procrastinating out of habit?

When I reflect on this, I think of our French Bulldog. She is built for both. One moment, she is still as stone. The next, she is launching into motion with surprising speed. It is funny and fitting—a little metaphor for the ways we all move through decisions and energy. We wait. We surge. And, ideally, we know when each is the right move.

Action and inaction both have a place. Leadership is not about choosing one over the other, but knowing when to lean into each. There is wisdom in the pause, and power in the pivot.

The point is not to move constantly. It is to move mindfully, and with intention. And that starts with understanding what type of moment you are in.

Are you responding to a reminder?

Or is it time to answer the alarm?

CHAPTER 8

Elbows Out

In leadership and life, you are not always given space. Sometimes, you have to create it.

If you are not willing to put your elbows out every now and then, the chances are that you will find that you are the one getting elbowed. That may sound blunt, but it is often true. The world moves fast. Voices get crowded out. Expectations stack up. If you are not intentionally carving out your place, it is easy to get overlooked, overruled, or pushed aside.

To be clear, putting your elbows out is not about pushing others down or dominating a room. It is not about volume, force, or taking space purely in order to be seen. It is about boundaries. It is about awareness. It is about having enough presence and clarity to make room for what you bring to the room, and to protect it when you need to.

Sometimes it means asserting your perspective. Sometimes it means holding your ground in a meeting or conversation where things are moving too fast or going in the wrong direction. Sometimes it is as simple as asking for a moment, rather than waiting for one to be offered.

Creating space is not about demanding attention. It is about choosing to value your own voice, time, and capacity, especially in environments that can consume all three.

I have learned that those who lead well do not always take up the most space. But they do know how to claim the space that they need. They know when to lean in, when to create room for others, and when to protect their own ability to think, recharge, or contribute in meaningful ways.

Leadership presence is not measured by how loud you are. It is measured by the steadiness with which you show up, and the clarity with which you hold your ground. Having your elbows out is not aggression. It is posture. It is poise. It is the quiet confidence to say, "I belong here, too."

So much of leadership today is about navigating crowded rooms, crowded calendars, crowded expectations, or crowded opinions. If you are waiting for someone to clear a space for you, you might be waiting forever. Sometimes, the space you need must be made, not found.

Put your elbows out when it matters. Make the room. Take the breath. Claim the space required for you to do your best work, and lead with clarity.

Because no one else can do that for you.

CHAPTER 9

The Power of Presence

In late 2022, I attended a Dave Matthews Band concert. One of the moments that stayed with me was their performance of "Sledgehammer," the Peter Gabriel classic, known for its energy and rhythm.

What stood out was not just the sound. It was the presence.

The entire band was locked in, moving and playing, fully immersed in the experience. They were not just delivering a song. They were giving something more. There was energy, connection, and a sense of joy that spread through the audience.

They played with precision, but also freedom. There was a little looseness, a little play, and plenty of trust among them. They knew their craft, and they loved it.

It reminded me how powerful it is to witness people who are not only good at what they do, but also clearly enjoying it. There was no hesitation, and no half-measures—just full engagement.

That kind of presence is powerful in any space, not just on stage. People can feel it when you care about what you are doing. They can feel it when you are energized, when you are invested, and when you are truly in the moment.

Joy does not have to be loud. It does not have to be announced. But when it is real, what it carries is projected outward. And when it is tied to purpose, it fuels performance in a lasting way.

That night, the music stayed with me. But what stayed even longer was the reminder: Energy and commitment are visible. And they matter.

CHAPTER 10

Order Up!

There are countless ways to build trust, and just as many ways to lose it. Whether it is with colleagues, clients, or the teammates we lead, trust is a fragile, powerful thing. And while I've seen trust built in boardrooms and on strategy calls, I've also found something simple, old-fashioned, and deeply effective, which is breaking bread together.

There's something about sitting around a table with family, friends, neighbors or teammates, sharing a meal and enjoying conversation. You learn things about people you never would through a performance dashboard or a scheduled meeting. So, I decided to take that idea further.

This wasn't about taking the team out for breakfast, although we've certainly done that, too. This was about something different. This was about preparing, cooking, serving, and cleaning breakfast for teammates with purpose, and at scale.

My first attempt was in Key West, the southernmost point of the United States. I packed two large coolers with everything I'd need: pancake mix, syrup, eggs, bacon, fresh fruit, coffee, juices, utensils, hot plates, cutting boards, chef's knives, serving trays… everything down to the paper towels. I hauled it all the way down to the branch, long before opening time.

The idea was simple, the team would walk in and see breakfast being made for them. Not catered. Not ordered in. Made with intention, and with care. It wasn't just food. It was effort. Effort they could see and feel.

I made their favorite breakfast items. I remembered who liked what. I did my best to cook it right, plate it right, and sit with them as they enjoyed it. And afterward, I cleaned up every dish. There was no fanfare, and no speech—just a simple act of service to say, "You matter."

There's a connection in moments like this. It's not about the meal. It's about what the meal represents. The time, the planning, and the effort—and doing all this without obligation or expectation—communicate something leadership books can't capture.

What started in Key West became a trademark for my leadership team. At our largest event, nine of us stood shoulder to shoulder over hot plates and griddles, preparing waffles, eggs, pancakes, bacon, sausage, and everything in between. Some of us brought homemade recipes. Some brought branded aprons. All of us brought humility.

One of the core rules I shared with the team was this; leave your ego at the door. This wasn't about being the boss. It was about being present. Serving others doesn't diminish leadership. It defines it.

These moments became more than meals. They became stories. Inside jokes. Memories with flavor. We still laugh about the questionable grocery bills and the chef hats from our "Key West Breakfast." But behind the fun was something lasting—a signal. It was a reminder that, when people feel prioritized, they show up differently.

The truth is that a morning spent reviewing numbers and pushing performance rarely leaves a lasting imprint. But a morning of connection, laughter, and sincerity often does. It especially does when it is with teammates who are tuned in to what leadership really looks like.

We don't always need to say more. Sometimes we just need to show up, set the griddle down, and start cooking.

CHAPTER 11

I Fix Appliances

Driving my son Dylan to school recently, I noticed a handwritten sign posted on the side of the road. It said only this:

"I fix appliances."

This was followed by a phone number.

That was it. No branding. No logos. No bold claims about quality, experience, or unbeatable pricing. Just three words and a way to contact them.

It made me smile because of how effective it was.

Over the years, I have spent time studying communication. From leadership seminars, coaching sessions, and books on messaging and influence, I have heard it said in countless ways. But it always comes back to a simple truth.

Say what you do. Say it clearly. Say it in a way that matters.

That sign did all of that. It cut through the noise. It did not try too hard. It did not overreach. It just told the truth.

And somehow, it stuck with me. I kept thinking about how often we overcomplicate our own messages. We try to make what we do sound more impressive or important by dressing it up in language. But in doing so, we sometimes bury the thing people actually need to know.

That sign felt like a blank canvas. It made space. It got to the point.

It made me ask myself a question. What is my version of "I fix appliances"? What is the simplest, clearest way to describe what I bring?

For me, the answer is this.

I ignite action that drives impact and success.

That is the through-line in my work. Whether I am helping teams find momentum, encouraging someone who feels stuck, or unlocking something that has not yet taken shape, my focus is to move people and ideas forward. That is what I care about. That is where I lead best.

Clarity does not limit us. It focuses us.

When we know what we do and how we help, it becomes easier for others to understand it, too. It becomes easier for our teams to trust, easier for our partners to align, and easier for our voice to carry in a crowded room.

So, the next time you feel the pressure to say more, to impress, or to over-describe what you do, pause and think about the sign I saw on the side of the road. It said everything it needed to say.

CHAPTER 12

Labels: Temporary or Transformative

Over the years, I have become more aware of the labels we carry. Some are given to us by others. Some we earn. Some we quietly assign to ourselves.

Recently, I overheard someone say, "That is above my intelligence." It was said casually, even with a bit of humor. But it stayed with me. The honesty in that moment was striking, but so was the finality of the statement. It felt like the door to growth had been closed.

It made me think about how easily we allow labels, whether self-imposed or handed to us to define us in permanent terms. We use phrases like "I'm not creative," "I'm not good with numbers," or "That's just not how I think," and repeat them until they become facts in our minds.

What if those labels are not facts? What if they are only temporary markers of where we are today, not where we are headed?

When we treat labels as endpoints, we stop looking for what might be next. However, when we view them as starting points, we leave room for growth. Knowledge, skills, and perspective are always within reach and often closer than we think.

In my experience, progress in this area usually requires two things.

First, we need the willingness to keep learning and growing. That includes seeking out unfamiliar ideas, making space for discomfort, and staying open to feedback.

Second, we need the courage to change the way we talk about ourselves. It is not enough to gain new understanding if we continue describing ourselves in outdated terms. The words we use shape not only how we see ourselves, but also how others begin to see us. Language matters.

This is not about pretending to be something you are not. It is about aligning your words with the direction you are moving in, not the place from which you started.

Over time, I have tried to be more mindful of the labels I hold onto. Some were useful at one time but have outlived their purpose. Others were never right for me to begin with. Letting go of them is not easy, but it creates the space to step into something new.

As you continue forward, this is a good time to ask a simple question.

What labels are you still carrying?

Are they helping you move forward, or quietly holding you back?

CHAPTER 13

Finding My Voice

At one point, I would not have guessed that sharing my voice online would become such a meaningful part of my journey. I had long trusted my voice in leadership with clients, colleagues, and friends. Whether in a meeting, a hallway conversation, or a conference room, I showed up with clarity and conviction. I was confident in those settings, where the responsibilities were clear and the relationships were familiar.

By contrast, stepping into a new medium, one where my words might be read out of context, where tone is easily misunderstood, and where feedback could be silent or sudden, felt different. It was unfamiliar ground. And I was unsure whether that version of my voice belonged there.

That started to change when a few people I trusted challenged me to engage more intentionally. They encouraged me to speak up, not for attention, but to connect. They believed I had something to offer, even if the format was new to me. They reminded me that, if my words could help someone in a meeting or a hallway, maybe they could help someone in a different format as well.

One friend in particular did more than encourage me. She asked honest, difficult questions. She wanted to know what was really holding me back—not just why I had not shared more, but why I believed my voice did not belong in spaces where others were already speaking up.

That conversation stayed with me.

Through self-reflection, steady encouragement, and a willingness to grow, I began to let go of some quiet hesitations. I began to write. I began to share. And I began to understand that what had been holding me back was not a lack of clarity or value. It was simply the unfamiliarity of being visible in a new way.

Taking that first step made all the difference.

The response reminded me of something important. People are hungry for real stories, honest leadership, and grounded perspective. Moreover, what we take for granted in our experience is often the exact thing that someone else may need to hear in their own season of growth.

The experience has reminded me that growth rarely feels natural at first. It often begins in unfamiliar places. It starts with people who challenge us to stop shrinking and start stepping forward, even when the space feels uncertain.

Finding your voice is not about volume. It is about honesty. It is about consistency. And, like a good swing on the course, it gets stronger with practice and intention.

Showing up with clarity, owning your perspective, and choosing to speak when it matters—that is what leaves a mark.

Your voice does not need to be perfect. But it does need to be yours.

Your voice is worth using.

CHAPTER 14

Who's Right?

There was a time early in my banking career when I believed that being a leader meant being right. I don't mean doing what's right, I mean proving, it. Getting the upper hand. Having the answer. Making your point land and making sure everyone knew it. I thought that was what I needed to do, in order to lead.

In those early days working inside the banking center, it was a lot to take in. A lot of moving parts. A lot of emotions, teammates, clients, and unexpected moments, plus an endless to-do list. I didn't know it at the time, but I was starting to compartmentalize. I was improving my skills when it came to tackling problems, staying in motion, and keeping it all moving. You do what you have to do to get through the day. However, sometimes, you start mistaking the things that help you cope with what helps you lead.

Back then, banking centers were handling a flood of fee-related complaints. That's a separate story in itself, but in short, emotions were running high. Clients came in frustrated, teammates were worn thin, and managers like me and many others had to balance it all. Somewhere in that chaos, I developed what I now know was a defense mechanism. It was a way of leading that sounded like confidence—but wasn't. I called it "who's right, who's wrong" leadership. And I got pretty good at it.

Someone would walk in fired up about a fee, a delay, or a misstep. Then, before the conversation even started, I was already sorting it in my head. Who's at fault? What policy can I point to? What line in the fine print will put this to bed? I had lines. Go-to phrases. I remember one in particular:

"Did you put it in your check register?"

Now, if you're reading this today, you might not even know what a check register is, and you'd be in the majority. But back then, it was a pretty standard way of managing your balance. So when I asked a client that question, I wasn't trying to help them. I was trying to pin the blame. I'd follow up with something like, "Are you keeping your balances up to date?" That was me saying, "This is on you."

I thought that was my job. I thought that was leadership—that the goal was to walk someone through a policy, prove they had made a false move, and move on. But I'll never forget the moment that illusion cracked, and how fast it fell apart.

A client came in. He was a doctor—tall, composed, and probably a respected member of the community. He had a quiet intensity and a way of looking at you that said, "I don't have time for nonsense." I had seen his account earlier that morning. I already knew the issue. Fees. A few of them. And I knew for sure he would be walking in to "hold court." I was ready. I had the facts. I had the timestamps. I had the policy. I was lined up to win.

From a policy standpoint, we were in the right. The bank

had done nothing wrong. But that's exactly what made the moment so revealing. Being right wasn't enough.

When he walked in that afternoon, he was calm but stern. We sat across from each other and I led the conversation, just like I had so many times before. I walked him through the activity. I pointed to the breakdown. I explained the fees. I told him why they weren't going to be reversed. I was polite but firm. By the end of it, he accepted what I would now regetfully call "defeat." He nodded. He didn't argue. But there was no peace in it. No resolution. Just… quiet.

I had won. But it didn't feel, like a win.

I looked at him and saw someone who was exhausted. Not just because of the fees. It was probably because he'd been pouring himself into his work—seeing patients, running a business, and trying to stay ahead. And now here he was, across from me, being told with a straight face that none of that mattered, that he had made a mistake and the bank was right.

And that's when it hit me. Being right hadn't helped. It hadn't solved anything. It hadn't built trust, deepened the relationship, or served the brand. It just made someone feel small.

Even worse, it had made me feel small. Because I could see, so clearly, that I had missed the moment. I had missed the opportunity to connect. I had been so focused on being right that I had forgotten why I was there in the first place. Not to correct. Not to defend. But to serve, to understand, to acknowledge, to create clarity, to build trust, and to lead forward.

I walked him to the door; as we reached it, he paused. He looked down at me, with a calm and direct expression, and said just a few words. I don't remember exactly what they were, but I remember how they landed. They weren't angry. They weren't sharp. But they made me feel like the smallest version of myself. It was not because he diminished me, but because he reminded me I had had a choice about how I made him feel.

That was the day I stopped being a transactional manager and started becoming a community-embedded leader.

It didn't happen all at once. It took more missteps—more moments where I caught myself slipping back into that old habit of trying to win. But I never forgot how hollow that win felt. And I never forgot the look on that man's face when I had been given the chance to make it better and hadn't done so.

Leadership isn't about being right, even when you are. It's about making it right. And more often than not, that starts with listening. I don't mean just listening to words, but to meaning. To what's being missed. To what's being asked for underneath it all.

Sometimes, it starts by saying, "I'm sorry you're dealing with this." Not because you're accepting blame, but because you're stepping into the moment with care.

That's how leaders lead.

CHAPTER 15

A Test of Limits, a Path to Growth

In Japanese tradition, Misogi is a sacred practice of purification a cleansing of the body, mind, and spirit that connects deeply with renewal and transformation. While it is rooted in centuries of cultural and spiritual significance, Misogi has become a powerful metaphor in modern life. It represents the kind of challenge that pushes us beyond what we think is possible, all in service of discovering who we really are.

My first Misogi was a 100.44-mile bike ride.

It was not just about physical endurance, though six hours on a bike certainly tested that. The real challenge, happened when I had a mile to go. The finish line was in sight. My body could continue. But my mind was done. Everything in me wanted to stop. I had proven my point, I had pushed hard, and I had already gone further than ever before. The voice inside me said, "You have done enough."

That is when I realized something important.

The hardest battles are not with the road, the conditions, or even our limitations. The hardest battles are with ourselves. They happen at the edge of enough—the moment when stopping is justified, but something deeper dares us to keep going.

When I reached the 100-mile mark, it was not just a win for the body. It was a renewal of the spirit. It reminded me that we are capable of more than we often allow ourselves to believe. The final stretch became a test of will, met by my own resolve and the unwavering encouragement of my fellow rider and family, who were there cheering me through the final half-mile.

Since then, I have committed to choosing one Misogi each year—a challenge that is not designed to impress anyone else, but to stretch the boundaries of what I believe I can do. It does not have to be physical. Sometimes the most difficult tasks are emotional, relational, or spiritual. The key is choosing something that requires full presence, effort, and belief.

Misogi is not about performance. It is about purification. It is not about the finish line. It is about the line you draw for yourself, the one that defines who you are before the challenge and who you become after it.

Like a waterfall carving its way through rock, our greatest challenges have the power to reshape us. They cleanse assumptions. They wear down excuses. And they leave behind a deeper understanding of what we are capable of—not just in moments of strength, but in the middle of struggle.

There is something freeing about going all in—about setting a goal that may not come with applause or attention, but that means something to you. About choosing discomfort, not for the sake of punishment, but for growth.

What challenge are you facing that could be your version of Misogi?

A Test of Limits, a Path to Growth

What would happen if you chose one test each year that made you reach beyond the comfortable version of yourself?

The question is not whether we are ready. The question is whether we are willing.

CHAPTER 16

Leadership, Doubt, and Owning Your Space

I recently watched an interview with Brian Johnson, the legendary frontman of AC/DC, in which he spoke about his early days in the band. I had already read parts of his memoir and had a sense of his story, but hearing him describe those early moments in his own voice made me want to understand more. I went looking to see if I could glimpse what he had been feeling.

That led me to a video of AC/DC performing "Thunderstruck" live in Newcastle, England (Johnson's hometown) in front of 70,000 people. The energy in the crowd was electric. His voice, one of the most distinct and powerful in rock music, was as commanding as ever. He owned the stage. If you only saw that performance, you would think this was someone with absolute confidence, born for that moment.

But in the interview, he revealed something surprising.

In those early days, he was terrified. He constantly feared he was not good enough. That someone would figure it out. That he would be fired from AC/DC because he just did not measure up. Behind the voice, the presence, and the sound, he quietly carried a doubt about whether he belonged.

That struck me.

I never imagined a rock star would wrestle with what we now call imposter syndrome—while performing on a global stage, in front of tens of thousands, with one of the most iconic bands in history.

And yet, I have heard that same quiet fear echoed in the voices of leaders across all industries. It is the worry that one day someone will ask the question they fear most: Do you really belong here? Are you really the one for this?

I believe the truth is this—most high performers feel this way at some point. It's not because they lack skill or grit, but because they care. They understand the weight of what they are doing, and they hold themselves to a high standard. That tension is real. And it is more common than most people admit.

And yet, they still lead. They still show up. They still step onto their stage, whatever that may be.

Two things matter above all.

First, do not let others define who you are. There will always be opinions. There will always be critics. But more often than not, the loudest voices are the ones doing the least. They are not in the arena with you. They are not carrying the weight you are. And they do not get to determine your worth.

Second, surround yourself with people who make you better. Mentors. Truth-tellers. Encouragers. People who are not impressed by your title, but are invested in your growth. You need people who see the real you—the you behind the voice. You need people who help sharpen your confidence, without inflating your ego.

Uncertainty is part of the journey. You do not have to

eliminate it. You just have to learn how to walk with it, without letting it hold you back.

Leadership is not about always feeling confident. It is about showing up anyway. It is about doing the work. It is about choosing to own your space even when doubt whispers that you do not deserve it.

Because if Brian Johnson can walk on stage in front of tens of thousands with that same voice in his head and still deliver thunder, so can you.

CHAPTER 17

Two Steps at a Time

At a recent conference, a colleague noticed something I did not think anyone had paid attention to.

"Aaron, you always take the stairs two at a time," she said with a smile. "I have seen you do it all week."

She was right. It is something I do without much thought, but it is intentional. With so much in our day that we cannot control, this is one of those quiet decisions that belongs entirely to me.

Two steps at a time feels like forward motion. It is not about being fast or trying to get ahead. It is a signal to myself. It shows that I am choosing to move with purpose—that I will meet the day head on.

That mindset often carries over into the way I work.

When a question comes up in a meeting or conversation, I tend to reach for the phone. A quick call or message tends to move things along faster than holding it for later. People still respond quickly, and even when they do not, a short follow-up often leads to the clarity we needed.

I picked up this approach while working with teams that

valued steady movement. The goal was not to finish everything in one day. It was to finish something. Keep things going. Do not let a good question sit still for too long.

Over time, I have also learned to appreciate other rhythms. Not everyone moves that way. Some people take more time by design. What once looked like hesitation, I now see as thoughtfulness. What once felt slow may actually be a deeper kind of care.

In my earlier years, I would step in when that happened. I would take the process, rework it, and hand it back. But I have learned to let people work in the way that gets them to their best outcome, not mine.

So yes, I still take the stairs two at a time. It is a small thing. But it sets a tone for how I want to move through the day. At the same time, I have learned to slow down when the moment calls for it. I have learned that not everyone will match your pace, and that is more than fine.

Progress is not about speed. It is about direction. It is about knowing when to lean in, when to wait, and when to trust the rhythm someone else needs to move forward.

That balance, the choice to move with intent, and the respect to let others do the same, is where the real growth happens.

CHAPTER 18

The Effort Behind Mastery

In one memorable meeting, I watched a leader stand before the room and create something powerful out of a single story. You could feel the shift in the room even before he spoke. Everyone leaned in, sensing they were about to hear something that would stay with them.

He shared an anecdote loosely attributed to Pablo Picasso.

A woman, thrilled to spot Picasso sitting quietly in a park, rushed over and said, "Master Picasso, I would be honored if you could create a quick sketch for me. Just something simple, but from your hand."

Picasso smiled, accepted the request, and quickly went to work. In less than a minute, he handed her a beautiful drawing.

"That will be 500 francs," he said.

The woman was stunned. "But that only took you 30 seconds to draw."

Without hesitation, Picasso replied, "No, madam, it took me 30 years to do that in 30 seconds."

That story stayed with me. I suspect it stayed with many in that room.

It captured something that is often hard to explain, especially in leadership. The simplicity, the clarity, and the confidence: none of it happens by accident. What appears effortless on the surface is almost always the result of years of dedication, repetition, failure, and learning.

We live in a world that often praises speed. But speed, in its highest form, is usually built on a foundation of slow, thoughtful work. Mastery does not come from motion. It comes from intention. It comes from time spent when no one is watching. It comes from the days you did not feel ready, but still showed up. Over time, all that effort becomes fluency. It becomes your voice. It becomes your way.

In leadership, this matters more than we admit.

The ability to create clarity, inspire others, or drive action is often mistaken for charisma or instinct. But more often than not, it is a product of deep work. The preparation you did weeks earlier. The experiences you did not know would teach you something. The discipline of listening more than speaking, and observing before reacting.

We are in a craft where no one ever truly becomes a master. That is what keeps it challenging. And that is what makes it meaningful.

That is why we must continue investing in ourselves.

The story of Picasso is not about speed. It is about the value of what is behind the speed. It is about the unseen work that gives weight to the moment.

So here is the question: How are you investing in yourself?

Not someday. Not when it slows down. Not when you have more time. Now.

The future version of you will one day need that 30-second

moment. When it comes, may your effort meet the moment with quiet confidence. And may others never mistake your mastery for luck.

CHAPTER 19

I Heard You, I Just Wasn't Listening

I used to make a habit of scheduling calls with teammates while I was driving between meetings or events. It seemed efficient. I had time in the car, and there were conversations that needed to happen. So I used that window.

But I started noticing something I could not ignore.

I am someone who needs to focus on the road ahead. Not just for safety, but for navigation. When I am behind the wheel, my mind tracks signs, exits, turns, and the rhythm of the traffic. Add a deep conversation on top of that, and it did not take long before I was blowing past the exits I needed.

That seemed harmless at first: a few missed turns, and a little delay. But the real issue was not where I ended up on the map. It was where I ended up in the conversation.

At some point, I began to realize something else was being lost.

A few conversations just felt off. I could not fully recall what was said or how it landed. Then a colleague asked me, gently, what had happened on a recent call. Why had I responded the way I did? Why had I seemed distant? I was confused. I thought I had been fully present.

But I hadn't. Not even close.

The truth was, I was 30 percent in the conversation and 70 percent on the road. And the person on the other end could tell.

That was the wake-up call.

I am a heavy notetaker—always have been. It helps me track not just what is said, but what matters. I listen closely, ask questions, and try to catch the moments that live between the lines. But when I was in the car, I was not doing any of that. I was hearing words but not absorbing them. I was speaking, but not responding with intent.

It was not about being rude. It was about being divided.

So I made a personal rule: If someone invites me into a real conversation, they deserve my full attention. That means no screens. No multitasking. And no calls while driving.

Many people would never know this. I do not advertise it. Some might say I still miss things now and then, and maybe I do. But I hold myself to that standard, because I know how it feels to be on the other end of a distracted conversation. You can feel it in the pauses, in the missed cues, and in the way it wraps up too quickly or lingers without direction.

Presence is not about making a big statement. It is about showing up fully for the person in front of you.

That starts with knowing where your focus is and being honest about where it is not.

CHAPTER 20

The Power of the Peloton

Not long ago, I found myself in a group setting where something was missing. Everyone showed up, the roles were clear, but the energy was off. People stayed quiet. The rhythm never caught on.

It made me think of something I have experienced on long rides, the dynamics of a peloton.

In cycling, a peloton works when riders take turns. Some lead from the front, others pull in the middle, and a few ride the rear, watching for gaps and helping the group stay tight. When each rider does their part, the group moves with a speed and efficiency that no individual could match alone.

However, when too many riders coast, even for a little while, the momentum shifts. The effort spreads unevenly. The group slows down, and small breaks in pace become harder to recover.

That group moment gave me the same feeling, the invisible drag when participation fades.

Galvanizing a group like that is not always about leading from the front. It might mean adding a small idea. Noticing someone's hesitation can help close the gap. Asking a question can help move things forward. Even a short contribution can change the pace for everyone.

During that ride, the power of the peloton was never about how strong each rider was on their own. It was about how willing they were to engage. The movement depended on shared effort and the understanding that momentum is something we create together.

In leadership, it is no different.

The strongest teams are not made up of performers looking to dominate. They are made up of people who notice the moment and choose to lean in, even briefly, to help keep the rhythm.

When we stop thinking about contribution as something big or bold, and start recognizing the impact of consistent, quiet effort, we unlock something better than speed. We unlock flow.

What keeps the group moving is not just the person in front. It is the shared decision to stay connected. To carry one another when needed. To play your part and trust that others are doing the same.

It is easy to forget that.

But every time I clip in and join a ride, I feel it again. And every time I step into a meeting or team setting, I try to ask myself one question:

Am I helping the group move forward, or waiting for someone else to pull?

It is a small question. But it makes a big difference.

CHAPTER 21

On the Side of the Road

Last week, I hit a pothole hard enough to take out both of my driver side tires. It happened fast, but it was the kind of moment that rewrites your day.

While I waited for a tow, I was expecting inconvenience. What I did not expect was a conversation I would still be thinking about now.

The driver who showed up was efficient and focused. But more than that, he was open. We talked while he worked, and somewhere in the exchange, I asked for his name and how long he had been doing this.

That opened the door.

He told me that, before the pandemic, he had owned a couple of trucks and run his own small towing company. He had built something from the ground up, something he was proud to own. But when Covid hit, everything changed. He was forced to shut down, and now he was working under contract for a larger company.

Twelve dollars per tow. That was what he earned, from start to finish.

When you consider the time, the fuel, the responsibility, and the physical toll, that number does not just sound small. It sounds heavy.

He talked about supporting his family of five, about his mother, who he hoped to bring closer to home, and about his desire to rebuild one day, if he could find a path to doing that.

I listened. And before we parted ways, I shared a few resources, programs, and tools that could help someone trying to reenter or restart a small business. He seemed grateful, not just for the list, but for the conversation.

Sometimes, connection starts with a simple question. Not a strategy. Not a solution. Just curiosity and care.

We often pass by people doing essential work, the kind that keeps others moving, without really seeing them. But when we slow down long enough to ask a question or offer something useful, that exchange becomes something more.

I did not meet an employee that day. I met a business owner in transition. A provider. A person with a story.

That kind of encounter reminds me why names matter. Why listening matters. Why sharing what you know, when it might help someone else move forward, is worth the time.

Not every day offers a grand stage for leadership. But most days offer a quiet chance to connect.

That might be enough.

CHAPTER 22

Powerful Moments

Some time ago, a new acquaintance of mine lost his wife after a lifetime together. I thought about reaching out, but since we had only met once, I worried it might seem out of place. Still, he crossed my mind often in the weeks that followed.

Then, unexpectedly, I saw him again in person. At first, I hesitated. I questioned the timing, wondering if offering condolences now would stir up sadness or feel misplaced. I was very much in my own head.

However, being the gracious person he is, he greeted me with a warm smile and a strong handshake. In that moment, I decided to say something. I offered a few words of condolence and shared a memory from our last encounter with his wife.

What happened next caught me completely off guard.

He pulled me into a hug. It was big, sincere, and deeply human. And it meant more than I can fully explain.

I had overthought it. I had waited, unsure of how it would be received. But what I had intended as comfort for him turned out to be comfort for me.

He reminded me what leadership looks like in its most honest form. It is not always about being strong or prepared. Sometimes, it is simply the ability to be kind. To receive connection. To offer grace, even while carrying grief.

Friendship, fellowship, and quiet support, no matter how new or unexpected, are the ties that help us move forward. We do not need long histories or perfect timing to make a difference. Sometimes, the most powerful moments come when we show up, speak from the heart, and lean in for the benefit of someone else.

Sometimes, that moment finds us right when we need it, too.

CHAPTER 23

The Shopping Cart

One of my mentors seared this lesson into my memory so deeply that it became a habit because it was the right thing to do, and because it worked.

I was out in the field with my leader at the time, visiting banking centers. I was excited: energized. I had our day planned to perfection, factoring in traffic patterns, time for conversation, observation, and even a few client interactions. It was buttoned up tight.

We pulled into our first stop, and I leapt out of the car, eager to share results and praise the team inside. I moved quickly, racing through the doors, ready to impress.

But after a few minutes inside, I realized… he had not followed me in. At first, I wasn't concerned. I'd been trained not to worry too much about capable people—they usually had a reason for being where they were. I began talking with the branch team, engaging in what I thought was a strong start to the day.

But minutes ticked by. And there was still no sign of him.

Eventually, someone looked out the front door and pointed. There he was. Coming down the walkway was my leader pushing a grocery shopping cart. It was filled with debris and trash. He was covered in sweat, still working. We watched as he stopped, picked up one last piece of litter, and guided the cart right up to the branch entrance. Without a word, he began transferring the trash into the branch's bins. No fuss. No frustration. He hadn't disappeared. He'd just noticed something I hadn't. This wasn't a "gotcha" moment. It was an "I got you" moment.

He wasn't really calling attention to what others had missed. He was showing quietly, and deliberately that standards mattered. This space, our space, was worth the effort. He didn't make it a about who had left the trash or why no one had picked it up. It was simply about doing the work that needed to be done, regardless of title.

The few people who tried to explain why the trash was there, and how it wasn't theirs were met with silence. No reprimand. No correction. Just an example.

From that day forward, I never again walked into a branch without first scanning the sidewalk, the parking lot, and the front door. It became instinct. And as we continued our market visits that day, you can bet it was a mad dash to tidy up each stop before he arrived. This was not because we feared him, but because he had shown us what mattered.

Over the years, I began to notice something else.

Show me someone with a disorganized back office, a cluttered teller line, or a forgotten storage room and I could almost guarantee that dual control, recordkeeping, or audit-readiness might follow suit. The way you maintain your space often mirrors the way you manage your responsibilities.

It turns out, leadership doesn't always announce itself. Sometimes, it rolls up quietly in the form of a shopping cart.

CHAPTER 24

Quiet Courage

Courage is another thing that doesn't always announce itself. Some of the most powerful forms show up without warning, without explanation, and without applause.

In both life and leadership, quiet courage carries more weight than most people realize.

It is the kind of courage that does not ask for a full plan before stepping forward. It does not need complete certainty before saying yes. It moves with conviction and a kind of trust that the next step is enough.

Dylan, our second child, has shown me that kind of courage more than once.

He does not hesitate when something new or unfamiliar shows up. A different sport, a steep ski run, or a new group of people. He listens, he considers, and then he steps in. Not to prove anything. Not to lead the moment. He just moves.

He says yes.

It is not careless. He puts real thought into his decisions. But the thinking does not stall him. It fuels him. I have seen him be the first to act, not for the sake of attention, but because the decision had already been made.

That kind of decisiveness stays with me.

Saying "yes" is not easy. It opens the door to failure, to discomfort, to the unknown. I still wrestle with it. I still find myself holding back at times, wanting more clarity than the moment can offer.

But leadership often begins right there. In the willingness to go before everything is certain. To speak when silence would be easier. To move when no one else has stepped in yet. That kind of courage, the kind that is steady and unshaken, changes the tone of a room.

Some of the best leaders I have worked with do not move loudly. They move with presence. They trust themselves and trust the people around them. They create an environment in which progress feels possible, even when the outcome is unclear.

Every strong team I have seen was held together by people who chose to go first. Not with all the answers, and not with bold declarations, but with a calm readiness to begin.

That kind of courage shapes the way I lead and the way I move.

It does not have to be loud. It just has to move forward.

CHAPTER 25

Something Just Fell

It was a football game at Hard Rock Stadium in Miami. My wife and I had settled into our seats, ready to enjoy the game. But just as things began, a commotion caught our attention.

Across the stadium, in the upper level of the end zone, people were standing, pointing, and shouting. Law enforcement was focused on something happening in the upper deck. From our position, it was unclear what was going on. Then I saw it, a small figure dangling precariously from the edge of the railing.

From a distance, it looked like a child. It was suspended awkwardly, with limbs flailing, dangerously close to falling. The energy in the stadium shifted instantly. The game, the noise, and the entertainment all faded into the background. Thousands of eyes locked onto one terrifying moment.

Fans rushed beneath the upper deck, forming a human net of sorts. Dozens gathered below, with arms raised, flags stretched, hoping to soften what now felt inevitable.

And then it happened.

The small object fell, flailing as it dropped nearly 50 feet toward the crowd below. A collective gasp swept across the stadium. The tension was absolute. People braced for impact.

And then, cheers.

But we did not know the full story yet. For nearly 20 minutes, we were left with nothing more than a blur of motion and an unclear outcome.

Eventually, the truth surfaced. It was not a child. It was a cat. Somehow, a cat had got loose and ended up dangling from the top deck. In a miraculous moment, fans caught it first in an American flag, then in a University of Miami flag, breaking the fall and saving its life.

The cat was unharmed. The crowd erupted in relief and disbelief. Laughter, cheers, and high-fives replaced the fear that had taken over moments earlier.

But what stayed with me was the moment before we knew. The moment when fear took hold based on what we thought we could see. The moment when our minds filled in the blanks, our emotions followed, and our hearts responded as if the worst had already happened.

It made me think: How often do we let incomplete information guide our reactions? How often do we believe the first version of the story and share it with others before we take the time to find out what really happened?

Do we circle back once we know the truth, or do we let the earlier version define the narrative?

As leaders, we are constantly asked to interpret situations, make decisions, and respond in real time. But we do not always have the full picture. We draw conclusions, we form opinions, and we sometimes lead based on assumption rather than fact.

This moment at the stadium reminded me how vital it is to stay open. To pause. To ask questions before reacting. It is not weakness. It is discipline. And it builds trust.

Perspective shapes everything. The more aware we are of that, the more easily we can lead ourselves and others through moments of uncertainty.

CHAPTER 26

Locked Out, but Not for Long

My daughter Abby went through a phase where she worried constantly about being locked out or locked in. At first, it seemed like a passing thought. But over time, it became clear that this was not just a moment of childhood uncertainty. It was a real fear for her.

She would ask repeatedly whether the doors were unlocked or whether she would be able to get back in. Her questions came with concern in her voice and a need for reassurance.

Rather than just talk her through it, I decided to take a different approach. We turned it into a learning project.

I taught her how locks worked. We practiced with basic lock sets and simple tools. We talked about the mechanics of a door, how it functions, and what to do in uncertain moments. We explored how surprisingly simple it can be to open certain locks, and we practiced techniques for staying calm.

She became a little locksmith in her own right.

And somewhere along the way, the fear shifted. Slowly, uncertainty gave way to understanding. Understanding gave way to skill. And skill brought confidence.

This was never about picking locks for fun. It was about replacing fear with knowledge and panic with preparation.

It reminded me that, sometimes, leadership means not just protecting someone from what they are afraid of. It means helping them face it directly, with tools, with support, and with enough space to learn for themselves.

Abby does not worry about being locked out anymore. She knows what to do. She knows how things work. And she knows she can handle it.

That kind of shift, watching fear turn into confidence, is one of the greatest gifts any parent or leader can give. Not just the fix, but the foundation. Not just the comfort, but the capability.

Leadership does not always look like having the answer. Sometimes it looks like handing someone the tools, showing them how things work, and staying nearby while they figure it out for themselves.

Sometimes, that is all it takes for the door to open.

CHAPTER 27

A Soldier's Manual

When I was young, my uncle was one of the few male influences in my life. Luckily for me, he was a true legend. His humor, sharp wit, and the way he treated me as an equal shaped my self-image. We laughed, we debated, and we built a bond that still grounds me today.

At the time, he was a soldier in the Army. One day, he handed me a small green book that he had carried with him. It was a worn copy of STP 21-1-SMCT Soldiers Manual of Common Tasks, Skill Level 1, issued in October 1985.

It captivated me.

I read it cover to cover, again and again. For someone like me, who had not served, this book offered a rare window into the systems, structure, and standards that shape the people who protect and serve our country. I was drawn not just to the content, but to the clarity. There was no fluff, and no wasted words: just precision, discipline, and direction.

Chapter 1 outlined the core of the Army's mission: to prepare soldiers to fight, survive, and win. It emphasized accountability, teamwork, and structure. The manual made it clear that every soldier had responsibilities, and those responsibilities had to be mastered. The expectations were high, and the measure of success was unambiguous.

What reshaped my thinking was how performance was measured. There was no ambiguity. Trainers had detailed criteria to evaluate each task. Soldiers were either observed directly or assessed based on outcomes. It was clear, specific, and rooted in action. You either met the standard or you did not. And that clarity, while firm, was never personal. It was about readiness. It was about responsibility.

That mindset left a lasting impression on me.

In leadership, we often hesitate to set clear expectations. We soften language to avoid discomfort. But that manual taught me that clarity is not harsh, it is respectful. When people know exactly what is expected, they are empowered. When feedback is tied to a known standard, it becomes a tool for growth, rather than a source of tension.

The Army's approach to development was systematic and layered. It was not about talent alone. It was about training. The manual introduced the idea of a "training ladder," outlining tasks at every level, collective, unit, equipment, and individual. Every layer reinforced the others, making the whole structure stronger. It showed that mastery is not found in isolation but in context.

There were diagrams and illustrations that brought tasks to life—everything from setting up equipment to moving with discipline in the field. It was not about theory. It was about readiness.

Over the years, that book has remained one of my most valued items. Not because of what it is, but because of who gave it to me and what it represents. It reminds me of the quiet power of preparation. It reminds me of my uncle's example, both in uniform and out.

He is still proudly serving. He is now a grandfather and still the same remarkable person who first handed me that book. His impact on me is woven into the way I lead, and the way I think about responsibility.

This manual may have been written for soldiers, but its lessons extend far beyond the military. Any leader can benefit from its principles. Discipline. Clarity. Practice. Evaluation. Integrity.

That is how you build people who are trusted. That is how you prepare them for pressure. And that is how you lead with strength and humility.

To all who serve and have served, thank you. And to my uncle, thank you for passing down something that continues to shape the way I move through the world.

CHAPTER 28

Preparation and Trust

Recently, I was catching up with a group of colleagues who had just arrived from the airport. One of them mentioned that takeoff always made them nervous. They worried that something might go wrong in those first few moments when the plane leaves the ground.

It made me reflect on how differently people experience uncertainty. For some, takeoff is a time of apprehension. For others, like me, it is a moment of excitement. The difference often comes down to trust. Not blind trust, but trust built on preparation.

When I fly commercially, I do so with confidence. Not because I believe nothing can go wrong, but because I know the people at the controls are prepared. The pilots, the flight crew, the mechanics, and the controllers—their training and precision give me confidence in the process, even when I cannot see what is happening behind the scenes.

This connection between preparation and trust became even clearer to me during my own flight training.

While I was continuing to build my aviation skills, I

experienced a training flight on which my Certified Flight Instructor tested my readiness by simulating engine failures. Several times during the flight, he pulled back the throttle without warning and said, "Unlucky for you, your engine just failed."

Each time, I responded immediately with the correct procedure: run through the checklist, scan for landing options, and calmly work through the problem.

Those moments were more than tests. They were reminders that preparation builds clarity. It does not eliminate the unknown, but it strengthens your response when the unknown arrives. The steps were not just memorized. They were understood, rehearsed with purpose, and practiced with intent.

That kind of preparation leads to trust—not just in flying, but in leadership.

In a business setting, the same idea applies. Are you the pilot, or are you the passenger? Sometimes we play both roles. We trust others to lead, and at other times, people trust us to guide the way.

As leaders, we need to recognize which role we are in and take it seriously. If we are leading, we need to be steady, composed, and deeply prepared. If we are following, we need to be thoughtful, curious, and confident in the people we have chosen to trust.

Preparation and trust are inseparable. One fuels the other.

When we are prepared, others can feel it. They sense the calm. They rely on our steadiness. And when people trust us, they are more likely to stay focused and composed, even when things feel uncertain.

The safest flights are not the ones where nothing goes wrong.

Preparation and Trust

They are the ones where the people are trained to respond when it does.

Leadership is the same. The strongest leaders are not perfect. They are prepared. And their preparation creates the conditions for others to feel safe, supported, and confident.

Whether it is in the air, or on the ground, trust is built through preparation. And preparation is proven not by what you know, but by how you lead when things are not going exactly as planned.

CHAPTER 29

When the Wave Hit

Many years ago, I was with my one-year-old son, Jake, in the gentle waves off Worthing Beach in Barbados. It was a quiet afternoon. Jake was sitting on my shoulders, laughing without a care in the world. The water was calm, and we had drifted out a bit farther than planned.

It was time to head back in. I turned toward the shore, still feeling at ease. But then, without warning, a wave hit.

It caught me off guard and knocked us both under. I inhaled seawater and began coughing, disoriented for a moment as I fought to regain balance. When I came up, holding Jake out of the water, I realized the wave had pulled us even farther out. The current was working against me. What had been a peaceful swim had instantly shifted into something more serious.

There was no one else nearby. No back-up. No help. Just the two of us and a sea that was no longer cooperating.

Then a second wave hit.

It was stronger than the first. I was tired, breathless, and still holding Jake above the surface. I could feel panic starting to rise. I tried to run through my options, but none of them felt good. I was slipping into trouble.

I made a decision that is still hard to talk about.

I took Jake off my shoulders and let him go into the water.

He could not swim. I knew he would go under. But I needed those few seconds. I needed air in my lungs, a moment to clear my head, and enough control to act.

He went under.

I pulled in two full breaths, got my footing, and reached for him. I grabbed him, held him close, and began swimming us both back toward the shore. There was no style to it. No grace. Just the steady slog of survival.

We made it back.

Jake was fine. He was too young to remember—too young even to realize what had just happened. But I have replayed that moment many times since.

Not every story like this ends the same way. Water is powerful, unpredictable, and unforgiving. Some families do not get their loved ones back. My heart breaks for those who know that pain. This is not just a story about a wave. It is a reminder of how fragile a single moment can be.

When I share this story, it is not for drama. I share it in the hope that it might help someone else pause, plan, or prepare. It might help a parent double check their surroundings. It might help a leader recognize that trying to carry everything, without a pause for rest, has its limits.

Because what I learned in that water applies well beyond the beach.

There are moments in leadership when we believe we can carry it all. We take on responsibility for everything and everyone, convinced that, if we stay strong enough, and focused enough, we can hold it all together. But the weight builds. The current shifts. The waves come.

And, if we are not honest with ourselves, we can slip under before we realize it.

In that moment, I had to make a decision. It was uncomfortable. It was imperfect. But it gave me the space to breathe so I could save the person who mattered most.

Leadership often requires the same thing. A moment to reset. A breath to clear your thinking. Sometimes the best way to protect others is to admit when you need a break.

It reminds me of something we hear every time we board a plane. Put on your own oxygen mask first, before helping others.

It is not selfish. It is essential. You cannot lead if you cannot breathe.

That day, Jake and I made it safely back to shore. But what stayed with me was more than relief. It was a quiet shift in how I saw responsibility. It was a hard-earned understanding that leading others does not mean sacrificing your ability to think, move, or breathe.

It means knowing when the moment calls for strength and when it calls for clarity.

At times, the hardest call is the one that brings you both safely home.

CHAPTER 30

A Leader, a Lesson, a Lasting Moment

During a recent trip, my daughter Abby and I had the privilege of a chance encounter with General Laura J. Richardson, a four-star general in the United States Army.

Abby, who has a strong interest in aviation and a clear sense of her aspirations, was excited by the opportunity to meet someone of such leadership, distinction, and global impact. I was just as honored.

When we crossed paths, I thanked the General for her service. Without hesitation, she turned her attention to Abby, engaging her directly with genuine curiosity and care. They spoke about school, favorite subjects, and aviation. Before we parted ways, she offered to take a photo with Abby—a simple gesture that meant a great deal to both of us.

I walked away from that brief conversation thinking about how powerful it is when a leader, despite great responsibility and stature, chooses to be fully present in the moment.

General Richardson is the 32nd Commander of the United States Southern Command, responsible for U.S. military operations across Latin America and the Caribbean. She has held several senior leadership positions, including Commanding General of the U.S. Army North and Legislative Liaison to Congress. In her distinguished career, she has also led combat operations with the 101st Airborne Division and supported mission-critical initiatives in Afghanistan.

It is one thing to read about a leader's accomplishments. It is another to see their values in action.

What stood out most was not her résumé. It was her ability to connect. Her willingness to make time for a young girl with a dream. Her instinct to pause, listen, and leave someone better than she found them.

That moment reminded me of the kind of leader I want to be: present, attentive, and grounded in service.

In a 2011 speech titled "Women's History in the Making," General Richardson shared this advice:

"Be confident in your profession, be consistent in your performance, and be committed. Take responsibility for your shortcomings and work on improving your weaknesses while maintaining your strengths. It all begins with a dream, a vision of what you want and where you want to go. Find that dream, then work tirelessly in pursuit of it.

"There are countless opportunities out there, including service to the nation, but none of them will be within reach without a clear vision of your path. It is the support and guidance from teachers, parents, coaches, and public figures that help make those dreams possible."

She lives that message.

Her actions with Abby were not a performance. They were real, thoughtful, and mindful. She was not just fulfilling her duty as a public figure. She was leading through presence.

That photo, now a keepsake in our home, carries more than a memory. It holds a lesson. Great leaders inspire not by reminding us how far ahead they are, but by helping us believe in how far we can go.

I remain grateful for that encounter. And I remain inspired by the example she set—in just a few minutes, with just a few words, and with the quiet power of being fully present.

CHAPTER 31

A Lesson in Success

During one of my visits to Barbados, I found myself watching the same man each morning as he entered the sea with nothing but a slingshot spear and a belt of hooks. No boat. No gear. Just him, the water, and his tools.

He would wade in alone and reappear some time later, with a fish skewered and hooked to his belt. It was quiet, efficient, and purposeful. There was no fanfare. Just results.

Eventually, I approached him. I was curious, not just about how he fished, but how he lived.

After a few questions, I asked, "Have you ever thought about taking tourists out with you? I bet they'd love it. You could turn this into a great business."

He paused and smiled.

"So you're suggesting I could build a business, grow it, and one day retire… and finally, just enjoy the sea and get my meal for the day?"

His response hit me in a way I did not expect.

He was not interested in building something more. He had already done that. What I was calling a starting point, he saw as the reward. He was not avoiding ambition. He was living in the result of it.

That moment reframed the way I think about success.

We often define success in terms of more. More scale. More growth. More visibility. But this man had found something different. He had already worked hard. He had already built his life. And now, he had chosen something quieter. Something more personal. Something that aligned with who he was.

It made me realize that success is not always about expansion. Sometimes it is about returning to the center. Sometimes it is about arriving at a point where you can choose your pace, live in rhythm, and enjoy what you have earned.

There is nothing wrong with growth. But there is wisdom in knowing when you have enough. And there is peace in knowing when your life matches your values.

This man was not trying to impress anyone. He was living in alignment with what mattered to him. And in that quiet clarity, I saw a form of success that is often overlooked.

Sometimes, success is not about building something new. It is about protecting what you have already built.

Sometimes, it is not about changing your life. It is about recognizing that your life already reflects what matters most.

What's your version of success?

And are you living in it, chasing it, or overlooking it?

CHAPTER 32

One Word

It is incredible how one word can unlock a flood of meaning, memories, and emotion.

Last week, someone said the word "sorrel," and my mind instantly returned to my Grandmother Joyce's kitchen, a place of warmth, tradition, and quiet love.

I used to help her make sorrel, a red drink made from the petals of the sorrel plant. At the time, I did not think much of it. It was simply a task. We added ingredients, tasted it, and then checked that it was at the proper stage. There was no rush. No shortcut. Just care. And process. Each step had its own timing, and she respected it.

Boiling. Cooling. Bottling. Days of preparation stretched before us. I often wondered why she made so much.

The answer became clear during the holidays, when family would gather at her home. Everyone would share a glass, listen to stories about that year's batch, and take bottles home to enjoy or give away. It was never just about the drink. It was about connection. It was joy, memory, and love poured into every bottle.

Even now, decades after her passing, I reflect on the care and intention she brought to every step. She was not just preserving a recipe. She was sharing a part of herself.

That memory reminds me that, when we give our time, knowledge, or traditions to others, we are doing more than completing a task. We are creating something that lasts. We are building something that may be remembered long after we are gone.

Whether in life or leadership, it is easy to focus on the result. However, it is often the care someone took in the process that people remember. The way something was done. The patience involved. The feeling that someone had put thought into every step.

My grandmother never used the word legacy. But she lived it.

She showed that leadership is not always loud. Sometimes it is expressed in quiet consistency. In showing up. In following through. In doing something well, not for recognition, but because it matters.

All of that came rushing back from one simple word.

CHAPTER 33

The Joy in Every Horrible Shot

Recently, I had an incredible time on the golf course, even though I was playing some of the worst golf I can remember. That may sound like an odd combination, but it was one of the most enjoyable rounds I have ever had.

My son was playing exceptionally well, finding rhythm and confidence with each hole. My father-in-law was showcasing the control and poise that comes from years of repetition and practice. Watching the two of them, one building his game, and the other refining it, gave me a unique appreciation for both the process and the generations behind it.

Meanwhile, my own shots were far from great. But something about that day was different. I was calm. I was enjoying the moment. I found myself smiling after bad shots, reflecting not on frustration, but on how clearly my results matched the preparation I had, or, more accurately, had not put in beforehand.

At one point, I said to my son, "If only my mental golf shots were reality, this would have been the game of my life." I could see every part of the swing I wanted, the ball flight, and the perfect drop onto the green. I had the vision, but vision alone is not enough.

That line has stayed with me.

It applies well beyond the golf course. In leadership, in relationships, in creative work, having the idea or the intention is not enough. Clarity of vision must be matched by the discipline to prepare, practice, and execute. Showing up unprepared and still expecting great results leads to disappointment, and sometimes confusion about why the outcome did not match the ambition.

And yet, there is value even in the off days. That round of golf reminded me that you can find meaning in the mess. You can learn from the imperfections. Sometimes the greatest growth happens when your expectations are not met, but your awareness improves. That awareness leads to better preparation next time.

There is a calm feeling that comes from knowing where you stand. There is peace in recognizing that results will reflect your habits, and that frustration fades when you focus on what can be improved.

The satisfaction of seeing preparation pay off is universal. You can feel it in a swing, in a meeting, in a decision, or in a team moving in harmony. Just like in golf, that calm moment before the shot often tells the story of what comes next.

Growth is not about perfection. It is about understanding the process, committing to it, and showing up fully, even when the outcome is not what you imagined.

Golf continues to teach me about patience and presence. It reminds me that joy can be found in the middle of struggle. Even the worst rounds hold lessons, if you are willing to pay attention.

CHAPTER 34

Humor, Care, and the Middle Seat

For years now, I have been intentional about how I show up, especially in rooms that carry weight. I try to bring three things: humor, vulnerability, and care. Not as performance. Not as distraction. But as tools that make the moment more real, and more human.

Humor, when grounded in sincerity, has the power to connect. A well-placed laugh can soften tension. A quick comment can open the door for conversation. Used well, it creates space for people to be themselves.

That awareness also reminds me of our middle son, Dylan.

He has a natural sense for moments. I have seen him walk into unfamiliar spaces and connect quickly, not by seeking attention, but by noticing what the room needs and offering it with warmth and ease. A well-timed comment. A flash of humor. A light moment that brings people closer, without ever pulling the spotlight.

That quality has shaped the way I think about leadership.

Some of the best leaders I know are not the loudest or most animated. But they give people room to breathe. They create an atmosphere in which others feel safe enough to be themselves, and steady enough to keep going.

Work brings pressure. So does life. Even with the best plans, there will be tough moments, missed cues, or long days that test patience and focus. A leader who can lift the room just enough, without losing the seriousness of the task, brings more than relief. They also bring clarity.

I have worked in places where the tone stayed heavy all the time, and others where expectations remained high but the energy was steady. In the latter spaces, people performed better. They trusted more. They stayed connected longer.

This is not about being funny. It is about being aware. Leaders who can read a room and adjust with intention are not softening the goal. They are clearing the path to reach it.

CHAPTER 35

Keeping Your Eyes Up

Cycling has taught me many lessons over the years, but one line from training stands out.

"It never gets easier. You just go farther and faster."

The more you train, the more your body adjusts. Your endurance increases. Your speed improves. What once seemed difficult becomes doable. But with that increase in pace and distance comes something else. You begin to move through new terrain. You cover more ground. And with that comes more to watch for, more to navigate, and more to learn.

Recently, I found myself reflecting on how this idea applies outside of cycling. I had been focused on the road directly in front of me. I was moving fast, hitting goals, and staying in motion. But I started to realize how important it is to keep your eyes up. Because no matter how efficient you are, if you are only watching the ground right in front of you, you can miss a hazard ahead.

Roads change. Directions shift. Hazards appear. And sometimes, the speed we are so proud of becomes the thing that blinds us to what is coming next.

Progress is not just about how fast you are moving. It is about how well you navigate. It is about awareness, adaptability, and staying connected to what matters most.

On the bike, you are taught to scan the road ahead, not just the front wheel. You are told to stay aware of your surroundings and to be alert to changes in terrain or traffic. The same principle applies to leadership. It is not always about staying in your lane. Sometimes it is about adjusting your position, shifting your view, and rechecking your direction.

The longer I have been cycling, the more I have come to appreciate three key ideas.

Keep your eyes up. The faster you go, the more there is to take in. Do not lose your view in the pursuit of speed. Awareness leads to better decisions.

Stay present. Do not become so focused on performance that you miss the people riding with you. Connection keeps you steady.

Embrace growth. There is power in learning and adjusting along the way. Some of the best lessons come while you are still moving.

Leadership, like cycling, is a balance of effort, focus, and awareness. There are times to push. There are times to coast. But in every case, keeping your perspective clear makes the journey more sustainable and more meaningful.

Speed alone is not the goal. The real measure is how well you see what is ahead, and how connected you remain to the people moving with you.

CHAPTER 36

The Illusion Of Leadership

I have been fortunate enough to attend some truly remarkable plays over the years, from small local productions to unforgettable nights on Broadway. The best performances pull you in completely. You are handed a program that sets the stage, the lights dim, the curtain rises, and for a few precious hours, the story feels real.

There is a rhythm to it. The anticipation before the show. The reflection during intermission. The final applause as the actors take their bows.

And then the lights come up. The performance ends. And reality returns.

Leadership, when it is genuine, is not a performance. But I have seen performances in leadership that rival any stage production.

Well-rehearsed speeches. Scripted enthusiasm. Carefully constructed scenes.

At times, it becomes hard to tell who is simply acting, who is willingly buying a ticket, and who is quietly questioning whether the show is all there is.

I have watched performances so convincing that they overshadowed the real work.

As a leader, you must resist the lure of the performance. The real work, the work without applause, without spotlights, is harder. It demands authenticity over accolades, and substance over staging. It demands that you stay rooted in reality, even when illusion becomes the norm around you.

Be careful. The fuel for these performances can be intoxicating—power, influence, and acceptance.

With enough repetition, indoctrination becomes normalization. The show becomes reality for some, but it remains fiction at its core.

You have the right to choose your path. You can stay in the theater, or you can step into the real world, even when it is harder, lonelier, and less celebrated.

Keep your head clear, your heart steady, and your pivot sharp.

I chose to write this chapter, not to challenge others, but to challenge myself. To stay anchored in the kind of leadership that is not rehearsed, and not polished, but real.

Today, I want to remind my team: Talking the talk can be enough to survive in some places. But it is never enough to lead.

Doing the work is essential. But even that is not enough anymore.

You must live it. Lead it. Mean it.

CHAPTER 37

Trusting the Process, Trusting the Person

The year had finally arrived when our oldest child was eligible to vote for the first time. Like many families, we were proud, but we were also thoughtful.

We encouraged him to participate and reminded him that the choice of how to vote, who to support, and what to believe in was entirely his. We talked about the issues he cared about, and we made sure the decision was grounded in his own values and perspective.

When I cast my first vote, I remember wanting to do it with intention. I did not want to follow someone else's guidance without understanding the reasons. I knew the impact of the vote was real, and I wanted to be thoughtful.

That same mindset is something I now hope to pass on.

Voting is more than a civic task. It is an expression of voice and responsibility. It is a right that was earned by generations before us and protected by those who serve today. And it is a way of shaping the future, not just for ourselves, but for those who come after.

I proudly cast my own ballot that year, and I quietly watched my son do the same. There was no speech, and no instruction. Just a nod, a quiet moment, and a sense of trust.

What stayed with me was not the act itself, but the space we gave him to make it his own.

Whether in your professional life or at home, leadership often means preparing others and then letting go. It means creating the conditions in which someone can make decisions with clarity, confidence, and ownership.

Not every moment needs direction. Sometimes the most meaningful leadership shows up in restraint, trusting the process and trusting the person.

CHAPTER 38

The Power of Being Seen

I once heard a story about a homeless man in a wheelchair who had fallen and gone unnoticed for some time. When help finally arrived, he was bleeding from a cut on his head, and one of the wheels on his chair had broken; that was probably what had caused the fall.

The team that found him cleaned his wound, helped him upright, and asked if he was in pain.

He began to cry, not because of the injury, but because someone had finally seen him. Someone had treated him with dignity, care, and kindness. That moment brought him something he had not felt in a long time. Joy.

It was not about the physical pain. It was about being acknowledged. It was about being treated as a person rather than a problem.

That story reshaped the way I think about presence and leadership. It reminded me of how powerful it is to simply see someone.

So much of leadership is about vision, direction, and decision-making. But some of the most meaningful leadership shows up in moments of connection. It happens when we notice what others have overlooked. When we take the time to listen. When we treat someone with patience, kindness, and respect.

We often think of recognition in terms of awards or titles, but recognition at its core is about presence. It is about saying, "I see you. You matter."

This is true in communities. It is true in families. And it is absolutely true in leadership.

The man who had fallen did not need a grand solution. He needed a human moment. And in that moment, his dignity was restored.

I think about how many people move through their day unseen. Not in a literal sense, but emotionally: overlooked, unheard, and unacknowledged. The impact of being noticed, especially in a moment of vulnerability, is immeasurable.

As leaders, we have the opportunity to make that kind of impact every day.

Not through speeches or strategy, but in how we notice the people around us. How we pause for long enough to listen. How we offer encouragement. How we show others that they are not invisible.

The power of being seen is not reserved for extraordinary moments. It lives in the ordinary.

We do not always need to fix something. But we can acknowledge it. We can show someone that their presence matters.

That kind of care leaves a mark.

CHAPTER 39

I Am Not Alone

Our daughter Abby was eight years old and preparing for a weekend equestrian competition. It was a two-day event with dozens of young riders, ponies in motion, and families gathered around the ring.

During one of the earlier rounds, a pony got spooked mid-jump. It threw its young rider, another girl about Abby's age, to the ground. Thankfully, she wasn't seriously hurt. But the pony bolted, running full speed around the ring in a panic. All the riders were told to dismount for safety.

The atmosphere shifted. What had started as a cheerful, high-energy event now carried a feeling of unease. The crowd quieted. Everyone was a little more cautious. And Abby's group was next.

Before she was called out for her round, we gave her a little extra encouragement. We told her how proud we were of her. With so many people watching and the pressure mounting, we wanted her to stay focused on her technique, and to hold her composure. I said how remarkable it was that she looked so steady and composed in the middle of that ring, all on her own.

She looked at me and said, without hesitation, "I am not alone. I have Misty."

Misty, her pony that day, had been with her through every jump, every training session, and every win. Abby didn't see herself as competing alone. She saw a partnership: a shared rhythm between rider and pony.

Her answer shifted something in me. It reframed what I thought I was witnessing and revealed how she stays centered under pressure.

It reminded me that strength doesn't require isolation, and that courage often shows up as connection.

In leadership, we tend to picture someone out front, carrying it all. But more often, the real work is shared with a teammate, a process, or a practice we trust. We are rarely doing it alone, even if it feels that way.

We all have our Misty: someone or something that moves with us through uncertainty. It might be a person. It might be a routine. It might be our preparation or purpose.

Recognizing that presence makes all the difference. It turns pressure into partnership. It turns fear into focus.

That day, Abby showed us what it means to stay grounded. Not by pushing through alone, but by leaning into what was already beside her. That season, she and Misty earned numerous championship ribbons, and they were also awarded a huge silver trophy for being the perfect pair.

None of us are meant to carry it all alone. Real strength often comes from seeing who or what is already with us.

CHAPTER 40

A Lesson in Expertise

In 2014, I visited a doctor, for treatment for arch pain. As he explained what I needed to do, I told him what I would follow and what I would skip. A bit surprised by my candor, he paused and said, "Aaron, I want to be clear with you. I am an expert at what I do. People come to me from around the world for my expertise and care. If you want to get better, you will follow my advice."

That reminder snapped me into focus.

I realized I was undercutting his expertise. I apologized, took out a notepad, and followed his plan exactly. It was difficult at times, but it worked. My arch pain went away. It never came back.

That moment has stayed with me. Not just because it healed something physical, but because it sharpened something mental.

It reminded me how important it is to listen to experts when they have earned that trust. And it made me reflect on my own leadership—what it means to be the expert in the room, and how to claim that space without arrogance.

Since then, I have often shared this story with teams and

peers. Not just to highlight the power of listening to the right voices, but to ask a deeper question: What are you an expert at?

When I ask that question, I usually follow it with silence. Let the person think. Let them answer. Let them wrestle with it if they have to.

Sometimes people answer quickly and clearly. Other times they hesitate. That pause tells me just as much as the answer does. It reveals either confidence, doubt, clarity or confusion. And often, the conversation that follows helps reveal what might have been sitting quietly beneath the surface all along.

If you claim you are an expert, you need to be. But you also need to say it when it counts.

Expertise is not just about what you know. It is about how clearly you communicate it, how consistently you deliver it, and how confidently others experience it.

That doctor did not oversell himself. He was firm, calm, and clear. And in behaving that way, he earned my trust. He also reminded me what leadership looks like when it is rooted in substance, not show.

We all have moments when we need to speak with that same clarity. Whether we are leading a team, guiding a client, or mentoring someone through growth, people are looking for steadiness. And when that steadiness comes from earned expertise, it makes all the difference.

Thank you, Dr. Hanft. Your care helped me recover. And your clarity helped me lead.

CHAPTER 41

Right Conditions

Hummingbirds have always fascinated me. They are extraordinary creatures, agile, graceful, and surprisingly elusive. For a long time, seeing one felt like a rare gift, a fleeting moment that you had to be lucky to catch.

But after redesigning the front landscape of my home, that changed.

The goal was simple: to bring more beauty, more nature, and especially more hummingbirds to the space just outside our window. I wanted to create an environment that was not only attractive, but also inviting. One that made the space feel alive.

Now, the hummingbirds come on a regular basis. They flit in and out, but they return regularly. What once felt rare now feels present, because the conditions have changed.

That realization reshaped the way I think about success. It reminded me that it often works the same way.

We chase it. We look for it. We sometimes wonder if it is out of reach. However, more often than not, success is not missing. It is simply waiting for the right conditions to show up.

And those conditions are almost always within our control.

To attract what we want, in life, in leadership, in our work, we must create an environment that allows it to arrive and stay. That takes more than good intentions. It takes action. You have to clear away what no longer works. You have to dig in. You have to plant with purpose, tend with care, and give things time to take root.

That doesn't mean it is about waiting around. It is about being deliberate.

Whether you are leading a team, nurturing a relationship, or building something new, the environment you shape will always influence the outcome. Culture matters. Tone matters. Systems, habits, and even the physical spaces we work in can invite growth or create friction.

People often say success is about showing up. I would add this: it is also about what you are showing up to face.

The preparation matters. The mindset matters. The space you create, internally and externally, has to be aligned with the outcomes you are aiming for.

This is not about perfection. It is about alignment. It is about being honest with yourself about what needs to change, and then having the discipline to make it happen, one step at a time.

Sometimes the transformation is gradual. You may not notice the change at first. But over time, the results become clear. Like a bird returning to the same branch day after day, success begins to feel less like something you have to chase, and more like something for which you have made room.

What you are seeking is not always far away. In fact, it may just be waiting on the other side of preparation.

CHAPTER 42

Every Drop Matters

This was a small lesson from my youth that stayed with me in a lasting way.

My mother and I were walking out of a grocery store when I dropped a penny. Without thinking, I kept walking.

"Aaron, aren't you going to pick up that penny?" she asked.

"No, it's just a penny," I replied.

She said nothing else in that moment, but I felt the weight of her silence. I turned around and picked it up.

When we got home, she asked me to do something unexpected. She told me to plug the sink, place the penny at the bottom, and turn the faucet on to a slow drip. Then she asked me to sit and watch.

At first, the drops seemed meaningless. Just a small, steady tap against metal. But slowly, the water began to build, into a shallow puddle, and then into a deeper one. Eventually, the sink filled completely.

There, at the bottom, surrounded by something much larger than itself, was the penny I had nearly left behind.

The lesson was simple. Small, consistent actions matter.

Over time, they build into something substantial.

That message continues to shape the way I think about leadership, personal growth, and building anything of lasting value.

It shows up in how we save. A few dollars at a time can lead to something meaningful. It shows up in how we build trust. Small moments of listening and encouragement accumulate into lasting relationships. It shows up in how we develop others. Steady investment leads to real growth, even when the impact is not immediately visible.

Sometimes we are waiting for the big moment. The loud recognition. The one breakthrough. But most of the progress actually comes from what we do when no one is watching. Quiet effort. Repeated intention. Belief in the value of consistency.

Leadership is often less about making a single huge decision and more about the tone you set over time. It is found in daily conversations, in small follow-ups, and in the care you bring to moments that others might overlook.

What looks like small change may actually be the beginning of something transformational.

I often think about that afternoon with my mom. She did not lecture me. She let the moment speak for itself. She simply created the space for the lesson to unfold.

From one drop to the next, that image remains vivid in my mind.

Every drop matters.

That is how savings are built. That is how confidence is built. And that is how trust is built.

Thank you, Mom. Your strength, your steadiness, and your ability to lead with grace shaped far more than you probably knew.

CHAPTER 43

Wider Views Await

There is an old Chinese proverb that offers a powerful image: "A frog at the bottom of a well cannot conceive of the ocean. A summer insect cannot speak of ice. A narrow-minded person cannot understand the way of the great Tao."

It is more than a poetic text. It is a reminder that our view of the world is shaped by the limits we place on ourselves. What we see, what we believe is possible, and how we understand others are all deeply tied to our willingness to look beyond what we already know.

When we stay in familiar places, routines, mindsets, and environments, we may begin to believe that the small patch of sky we see is all there is. Our perspective becomes narrow, not because we lack intelligence or drive, but because we have stopped reaching. Comfort quietly becomes confinement.

But the world is not confined to the circle of light above the well. Nor are we.

Growth begins when we look beyond the boundaries we have accepted. It takes shape when we explore new conversations, take on new challenges, and allow ourselves to be changed by unfamiliar experiences. It begins when we recognize that the ocean exists, even if we have never seen it; that ice is real, even if we have only known summer; and that there are deeper ways of understanding, even if we have lived in the shallows.

It is easy to say we embrace growth when the changes are on our terms—when we feel in control, when the change makes sense. But the most genuine kind of growth rarely arrives that way. It often shows up as discomfort, uncertainty, or something that pulls us outside what feels reasonable or familiar.

That moment, the stretch into unfamiliar space, is where transformation lives.

True growth is not measured by how far you go geographically or how different your role becomes. It is measured by how much more you can see, and how deeply you can think. It is measured by your ability to return from that stretch with something new to offer, a sharpened mind, a steadier spirit, or a wider view.

When we bring back fresh energy, new awareness, or deeper clarity, we are not the only ones who change. We also become agents of change for others.

The most impactful leaders I know are not defined by where they have gone, but by how much they have seen. They are the ones who stepped climbed out of the well, and, instead of being disoriented by the size of the ocean, became inspired by its possibility. They are the ones who came back with open hands, new language, and a spirit that was ready to help others grow as well.

This is not a call to abandon what you know. It is a call to see beyond it. To be curious. To stretch. To imagine that more exists, in yourself, in others, and in the world around you, than what is currently in view.

The goal is not to return the same. The goal is to return changed.

Wider views await. We simply have to look up, and be willing to climb, and bring something back that helps others see more too.

CHAPTER 44

The Room Was Watching

One of the moments that has stayed with me happened in a room of 125 leaders. It involved a simple golf mat, a Scotty putter, and one of my teammates, Angela.

We were gathered for a leadership meeting, and I wanted to demonstrate something that often gets overlooked. We say we are here to lead, to grow others, and to elevate performance but what does that actually look like?

I rolled out a putting mat in the center of the room, placed a golf ball down seven feet from the hole and stood up with the putter in hand. Then I asked, "Who would like to volunteer to make this putt from seven feet?" Angela, who was sitting near the front, immediately raised her hand.

She had never played golf before. That made her perfect for what I wanted to show.

I handed her the putter and gave no technical instruction. Just the putter and the ask.

As she set herself to make the shot the best she could with no guidance, I related this to asking our teammates for whatever this week's goals were and expecting great results. Well, Angela missed—and that was the point.

I started her at the longest distance intentionally, because that is what many of us do as leaders. We begin with the big ask. We set a stretch goal. We aim far and tell people to get there. But without the right tools, clarity, or support, even the most willing teammate can fall short.

That's when we reset.

I walked over, crouched beside her, and spent a few minutes walking through the basics. I showed her how to grip the putter. I demonstrated the pendulum motion smooth and steady. We talked about alignment, keeping the face square, and using the lines on the mat to guide her swing. I did all this on the microphone, not to spotlight her, but to ensure the room could follow the lesson in real time.

Then I moved the ball to the three-foot mark. I wanted her to experience success. I wanted her to feel what it was like to connect and for the room to see what was possible with just a bit of guidance and belief.

She lined up and sank the first putt. The room was surprised and applauded warmly.

I placed a second ball at the same mark. She made it again. The clapping grew louder, more excited.

Then I placed the third ball at five feet—this would be more difficult, but now she had confidence on her side.

She took her time, focused, and made the putt.

The room exploded.

Leaders jumped to their feet. Some of them even high-fived. It had become something more than a simple demonstration. It had turned into a collective moment—a visible shift in belief and energy.

Now if you must know, I had no idea whether any of this would work and I almost did not go for the five foot putt. However, I realized that, as the leader, I needed to trust in the process and, more importantly, the people, in this case Angela.

That moment was never about golf.

It was about what happens when, as leaders, we step in with presence and clarity. When we take the time to teach instead of just assigning tasks. When we move from asking for more, to building the foundation that actually makes more possible.

Supporting people does not mean standing back and cheering. It means getting close enough to guide and steady them. It means offering the tools, showing how to use them, and then stepping back to let someone grow.

Angela reminded all of us that day; before the ask, there must be the investment. Before we expect someone to reach farther, we must help them feel what it is to succeed at closer range. Build the skill. Build the confidence. Let them repeat it. Then stretch.

That is how progress takes root. That is how belief is earned.

For leaders, that is the part we cannot skip.

Together, we grow.

CHAPTER 45

The Guidance Gap

In leadership, one of the most important roles we play happens just before someone takes a leap. A teammate stands on the edge of something new—a promotion, a move, or a meaningful shift—and they're hopeful, excited, and committed. You may have helped shape the path to get there. You're proud. You're in their corner. You also know something else: No matter how well it's planned, life is going to happen.

It's easy in that moment to move forward quickly, to celebrate, and to shift attention to the next priority. The opportunity is set. The next chapter is calling. It's tempting to feel like your part is finished.

But this is where leadership still matters—maybe more than ever.

There's often a brief window where we can add real value. Not by slowing someone down or raising concern, but by helping them prepare with intention. I've come to think of this window as the guidance gap—the space between decision and lived reality. Energy is high. The story in their head is fully formed. Yet there are parts of the journey that haven't been surfaced or named.

This is not the time for warnings. It's a time for reflection. A time to ask better questions, and to listen closely for what hasn't yet been said.

A few thoughtful questions can go a long way. What are you picturing this looks like a few months in? What part of this excites you most? What part makes you hesitate, even slightly? What would make this transition feel not just successful, but supported?

Most importantly, ask: What do you need from me right now? What kind of support would be helpful from me as you make this move?

Sometimes, those conversations confirm that the timing is right and the direction is clear. Other times, they reveal a few assumptions that deserve more attention. Once in a while, they spark a shift—not in the opportunity itself, but in how your teammate steps into it.

That kind of clarity isn't just helpful—it's healthy.

I've had the privilege of seeing many people grow into new roles, take on new challenges, and step into leadership. These are the moments we work toward. They deserve to be celebrated.

Still, I've also witnessed what comes after. Roles that shift unexpectedly. The weight of new responsibilities. The strain of timing or relocation. Those experiences don't make the move wrong—they just remind us that even great decisions carry real impact.

As a leader, your role is not to prevent the friction. It's to make sure they don't go through it alone. The way you show up now sets the tone for how they'll process change, manage doubt, and build trust in what's next.

This is also the right time to help them transition their momentum into the hands of their new leader. You can encourage them to carry forward the insight from your time together. What they're most proud of. Where they've stretched recently. How they like to be led. What they're still figuring out. That isn't holding on—it's handing off. Thoughtfully, fully, and in a way that honors the work done on both sides.

The guidance gap isn't a moment to second-guess. It's a moment to slow down with care, and to support someone not just with encouragement, but with presence and perspective.

That's leadership. Not correction. Not control. Just clarity. Just commitment. Just a willingness to help them step forward with strength—and stay connected, even once they do.

CHAPTER 46

Humble to a Fault

Over the years, I have had the privilege of leading many teams across many markets. One thing I've noticed is that teams often start to reflect the traits of their leader. Sometimes it's in their discipline. Sometimes it's in how they communicate. Sometimes it's in how they carry themselves in moments of recognition.

For many years, one of the traits I valued most was humility. It came naturally to me. It shaped how I spoke, how I led, and how I celebrated the work of others. It served me well in a lot of ways. In many ways, it still does.

A few years ago, something shifted. I began to notice something subtle, but real. Being humble was starting to cost my team.

The people I led were producing incredible results. Their performance was strong. Their intent was clear. Yet their names were not being mentioned. Their efforts were not being seen. Their impact was not being shared. They were too quiet about it.

They assumed the work would speak for itself. They believed that showing up, doing the job, and helping others would be enough. For a long time, I believed that, too. I no longer do. Today, I believe that if you remain humble to a fault, you will be left behind.

This doesn't mean becoming loud or self-promotional. It doesn't mean chasing every spotlight or grabbing every credit. What it does mean is protecting your work. Taking ownership of your impact. Documenting, communicating, and reflecting on what you've done and how you did it.

Failing to do so leaves the door open for someone else.

The modern workplace rewards visibility. It is filled with people who are quick to attach their name to something that looks successful. While that doesn't make them bad people, it does create risk for those who build quietly and never raise their hand.

I've seen careers rise based on the momentum of someone else's effort. I've watched individuals expand their reputation by pointing to results they didn't create. I've seen the people who actually did the work left wondering what happened.

Not every case is malicious, sometimes the credit is simply sitting there unclaimed. It looks like free space. It sounds like an open idea. It feels like no one owns it. So someone claims it—not because they earned it, but because no one else did.

This is what happens when humility goes unchecked.

So my updated message to leaders, and to those they lead, is this. Teach your people to protect their work. Encourage them to speak clearly about their contributions. Show them how to reflect their impact in midyear reviews, team calls, casual conversations, and one-on-one updates.

This is not selfish. It does not undermine collaboration. It ensures the credit follows the work. It makes sure value is not

Humble to a Fault

separated from the person who created it.

Celebrating outcomes together is good. Watching someone else's name ride on what you built—because you stayed silent—is not. If you lead, lead in this area, too. Stamp your name on it, follow up on it, speak to it and connect your voice to your effort. That isn't pride. That is responsibility.

The goal is not boastfulness. The goal is clarity. If you are the one doing the work and say nothing, at some point it's not humility. It's allowing it to happen.

There are peacocks in every company. People who strut with borrowed feathers. People who have mastered the art of show without the skill of delivery. They shine because no one interrupts the illusion. That's on us and failing to protect your own work—or failing to guide your team to protect theirs—leaves performance open to mislabeling, misplacement, or erasure.

I still believe in humility. Now I believe it must be paired with ownership. Humility without clarity becomes a liability. You can be a strong teammate. You can be a great collaborator. You can uplift others and still name what you've done.

That isn't arrogance. That's leadership. If you want your leadership to last, your voice must travel with your work.

CHAPTER 47

Questions You're Not Supposed to Ask

There are rules, and then there are instincts. I've always believed in the rhythm of relationship-building—the idea that in banking, especially when working with small business owners, there's a certain way to approach people. You move with care, ask polite questions, and earn the right to go deeper over time. That rhythm becomes almost sacred, a learned respect for the natural pace of connection.

Someone on my team challenged that thinking. She was sharp, curious, and had an uncanny ability to uncover highly specific business information—often within minutes of meeting someone. I was continually amazed by the detail she surfaced: key financials, tax positioning, loss history, even insurance structures. What stood out even more than what she discovered was how quickly she got there.

She asked questions that most professionals would avoid in a first meeting. Not because she was aggressive, but because she didn't realize those questions were typically considered off-limits—not in the way I had been taught, at least.

I remember one meeting in particular. Within the first few

minutes of sitting down with a business owner, she asked a tax-related question that many seasoned advisors might approach only after several meetings. I felt myself wince, thinking it might land the wrong way. We had barely introduced ourselves.

However, the business owner didn't hesitate. He answered clearly and comfortably, and the conversation moved forward with ease and professionalism.

During our debrief, I asked how she felt about the pace of her questions and whether she thought any had come across too strong. She looked at me—genuinely, without a hint of defensiveness—and said, "I didn't bend their arm. I just asked. They gave me the answer."

What I realized and learned in that moment is that urgency without arrogance is rare—and valuable.

She wasn't racing through the conversation to prove herself or chasing numbers to close a deal. Her pace came from understanding something I hadn't fully considered: When a small business owner agrees to meet, that window might not stay open for long.

If someone is sitting down to talk finances, it often means the need is real, time is limited, and a solution has to follow quickly. Her mindset was clear—get to what matters, because if you can help, help now.

Her questions weren't intrusive—they were efficient. The urgency wasn't pressure—it was purpose. And when the moment called for slowing down, she adjusted naturally.

That approach taught me something important. I had been holding tightly to what I believed was the "right" way to engage, thinking I was protecting relationships by sticking to the traditional rhythm. But what she showed me was something else—she was honoring the moment, not the method.

In fast-paced environments where time is short and needs are real, I've come to see that urgency and respect can absolutely coexist. Sometimes the most important move is not to wait for the perfect time, but to ask the question that gets the conversation where it needs to go.

I've carried that lesson forward. Not because I've changed my values, but because I've expanded my perspective. Asking bold questions isn't about showing off—it's about being helpful. It's about understanding quickly so you can serve well.

Leadership means staying open to new approaches, even when they challenge what you've always done. I'm grateful for what I saw that day and for what it reminded me: Don't confuse etiquette with impact. Don't assume someone's pace means they're pushing. And don't overlook the value of moving with purpose—especially when the moment calls for it.

CHAPTER 48

Delray Beach

Some leadership lessons don't show up in slides, handbooks, or training sessions. They arrive unexpectedly—in the form of heat, discomfort, and a challenge you didn't see coming.

Our team had gathered for an off-site retreat at our leader Mike's home in Delray Beach. It was a generous gesture—not only in the invitation, but in the thoughtfulness behind it. Mike and his wife welcomed us with kindness, offering a tour of their home before the day began. Just a mile from the ocean, the setting gave us a chance to step away from the usual grind and reconnect in a more personal way.

The group included senior leaders from across South Florida. Each of us was experienced, performance-driven, and deeply familiar with the business—and with one another. This gathering felt different from the start. The structure of hierarchy fell away. It wasn't about metrics, reviews, or outcomes. It was about learning something else, though none of us yet knew what.

We were told we'd be paired up and given a list of ten tasks to complete across town. Each team would be judged on two measures: how many tasks were completed, and how quickly they returned. There would be two teams recognized—one for speed, one for completion.

The moment the instruction sheets were handed out, something shifted. What began as relaxed conversation turned quickly into movement. Some glanced at the list; others didn't. Everyone headed straight for the door. The South Florida heat met us immediately—heavy, unrelenting, near 100 degrees. What was meant to be a bonding experience became something more physical, more pressing.

I partnered with a teammate I knew well—steady, sharp, brilliant under pressure. We'd handled countless high-stakes situations together, though never quite like this. With no map, no real plan, and no idea what the other teams were doing, we jogged into town following the first signs of motion.

At one point, I said, only half-joking, "We could turn around right now and probably be the first ones back. Zero points, but best time." The idea was funny, tempting even, but we kept going.

The first major stop brought us to the beach. There, we were handed small plastic buckets filled with holes and instructed to fill them with ocean water, run them up the sand to a marker, and repeat. It quickly became clear this wasn't a one-time task—it was a full effort challenge. People tried stacking buckets to slow the leaks or plugging holes with their fingers, but most of us just ran, dropped water, and came back for more.

That was just one item on the list.

We completed seven of the ten assignments—not a bad showing, though we were among the last to return. By then, everyone was hot, sunburned, a little disoriented, and maybe slightly confused by what had just happened.

Then came the debrief.

There was no criticism or scoring breakdown. Instead, Mike invited reflection. What became immediately clear was that no team had stopped to make a plan. No one had discussed proximity, point value, route strategy, or team roles. We had all defaulted to movement before alignment.

It was an exercise in self-awareness—one that didn't need to be explained to make its point.

That afternoon gave us a mirror. We saw our strengths: our bias toward action, our comfort with urgency, our ability to adjust under pressure. But we also saw the cost of skipping alignment. The experience wasn't about right or wrong—it was about pause. It reminded us that sometimes our best instincts can carry unintended consequences when left unchecked.

Over time, I've returned to a few key lessons from that day:

- Planning isn't wasted time. A short alignment up front saves rework later.
- Knowing your team is essential. Just as important is helping your team know itself—how it functions, what it misses, and what it leans on too heavily.
- Some of the best development moments come when people feel the discomfort firsthand. Telling doesn't land the same as experiencing.
- Group dynamics shift. As leaders, we must revisit those dynamics often, with fresh eyes and honest feedback.
- Momentum without intention can drain energy. Moving fast is only useful when it's paired with clarity.

There's one more that stands out most clearly: Leadership isn't just about getting a team moving. It's about knowing when not to move. It's about pausing long enough to ask a better question—before jumping to the answer.

What mattered most that day in Delray wasn't the list or the pace. It was the clarity that emerged when the day was done. That clarity didn't just inform how we led. It changed how we showed up the next time a new challenge appeared.

CHAPTER 49

Encore

I was watching a performance by a wildly popular band, playing one of those songs that just pulls you in. Every beat was in place. Every note felt right. It sounded flawless.

But just as the final chord rang out and the audience responded, the lead member of the band calmly brought everything to a stop. There was no anger or frustration, just a clear message: "That wasn't it."

Without hesitation, they started the song from the top. It wasn't dramatic or performative. It was grounded. The rest of the band didn't flinch or show a hint of hesitation. Just from the top.

That moment offered something rare, a window into the discipline behind excellence. A reminder that even after years of repetition and success, a team can still hold itself to a standard beyond applause. It was not about chasing perfection, but being committed to something more honest. It made me reflect.

In leadership, how often do we keep moving because things look good enough on the surface? Because stopping feels inconvenient? Because calling something out in real time might create discomfort?

But there's a certain kind of courage in saying, "That wasn't it," and choosing to reset.

I've had moments where the outcome was technically right, but the process behind it wasn't clean. There were also times where the message was delivered, but not received in the way we intended. And there were moments when something was close but not aligned with the standard we had set for ourselves. The easy path is to let it go—to move on and not disrupt the rhythm. But sometimes, the most powerful thing a leader can do is pause, name what's off, and go again. Not for show or ego but because it matters.

When it's done with clarity and care, it teaches something quietly profound; that what we do and how we do it deserves our full attention.

CHAPTER 50

Owning the Feedback

One of the greatest tests of leadership is how you respond when the truth is uncomfortable.

At one point in my leadership journey, I was supporting a large number of teammates across a broad region. With tens of thousands of client touch-points every day and teams operating across many locations, feedback became a critical part of how we led.

Like most organizations, we valued feedback. We encouraged it, measured it, and responded to it. Some came through formal surveys. Others arrived through mystery shops or internal reviews. Each piece gave us a chance to step back and assess what we were doing well—and where we needed to improve.

For a period of time, the volume of feedback coming in was unusually high. Month after month, our leadership team reviewed comment after comment. Some were uplifting. Others were critical—sharp enough to make even the most seasoned leaders shift in their seats. Still, we stayed with it. We studied the themes, identified the gaps, and acted on what we could. We also made a point to highlight and protect what was working well. Feedback should never only be about what's wrong. It should also help preserve what's right.

What stood out most wasn't the feedback itself, but the reaction to it.

When a difficult comment was read aloud, the first question I often heard was, "Was that my area?" The concern was real. Once someone realized the comment didn't apply to their location, you could almost see the exhale. The tension left their shoulders. The pressure felt momentarily lifted.

When the comment was about their area, the shift was immediate. People moved into explanation mode—describing the circumstances, referencing the teammate involved, or suggesting the client might have misunderstood something. It was rare to see someone simply pause and take it in without the instinct to create some distance.

That's when I changed the approach.

At our next meeting, I removed all identifying details—office names, location codes, even manager initials. Then I invited not just leaders, but teammates from all levels to be present as the comments were shared aloud. In most cases, I read them myself or had one of our next-level leaders walk through the feedback with the group. The goal wasn't to assign blame or spotlight anyone—it was to hear the voice of the client clearly. Without filters. Without distraction.

Everything shifted.

Without knowing where the feedback had come from, no one could disconnect. The comment could have been about anyone's office—or any one of us. It created a shared sense of presence, like the client was in the room. Whether the feedback was worth celebrating or difficult to hear, it became real.

Owning the Feedback

The praise mattered just as much as the critique. When clients called out great experiences or mentioned teammates by name, we didn't let it sit on a report—we read it out loud. We made space to feel what those moments meant. Teammates saw their effort reflected back in front of their peers, and leaders could witness the direct result of high standards and care. Celebrating wins publicly wasn't just feel-good—it was strategic. It taught people what excellence looks like, and it helped us preserve what we never wanted to lose.

I watched the energy shift from avoidance to ownership. The conversation moved from "Is that us?" to "What can we do with this?"

That moment became a turning point. We called it owning the feedback.

It wasn't about blame. It was about staying open. We used it not just to fix gaps, but to preserve what mattered most. When client comments consistently praised a particular experience, we studied how to keep it strong. When we planned operational changes, we considered whether those changes might affect something clients clearly valued.

Even our discussions with senior leaders became sharper. We weren't reacting in silos—we were aligning around the same signals. With teams across multiple offices responding to the same insights in the same way, the patterns became clear. The action steps became faster. The unity became real.

It's easy to talk about growth in theory. Again and again, though, it shows up in the smallest, quietest moments—the way we listen, the way we respond, the way we choose to own what's hard.

Progress doesn't require the perfect system. It requires the mindset to face what the system reveals.

Feedback only works when we choose to engage with it—fully and honestly. That includes the uncomfortable moments. The comments that sting. The words that make us want to explain, excuse, or ignore.

Results are easy to own when everything looks good.

What defines us is how we own the feedback too. Even when it's hard. Especially when it's hard.

That's the work. Always worth doing.

About the Author

Aaron Patience writes from experience, not theory. After 30 years leading teams and helping people grow, he believes leadership is shaped in the decisions we make, the pressure we carry, and how we show up when others need us most. His work focuses on helping others get better—not by chasing perfection, but by improving steadily through each challenge, conversation, and choice.

His stories are grounded and reflective. They come from the field and everyday life. With clarity and care, he writes about the kind of leadership that lasts—honest, practical, and built to stick. His approach encourages forward movement, reflection, and a commitment to what matters.

Born in Trinidad and Tobago, but based in Miami, Florida, Aaron often retreats to Barbados with loved ones to relax, reflect, and reconnect. For over twenty years, he and his family have been part of the close-knit community at Riviera Country Club in Coral Gables—a place that continues to offer grounding, perspective, and community. These places—each in their own way—have shaped how he leads, reflects, and connects with others.

He enjoys traveling with his wife and three children, playing golf and tennis, photography, and flying. A passionate aviation enthusiast and student pilot, he finds meaning in both the altitude and the everyday.

Leadership Impact is the first in a growing series for those committed to leading with care, clarity, and purpose.

Acknowledgments

This book came together over the course of a year, but the lessons and stories inside it have been shaped over a lifetime—by people who challenged me, supported me, and helped me grow. I'm grateful for each one of you.

Vanessa—For your love, support, caring, clarity, and patience.

Jake, Dylan, and Abby—You are the center of it all. You keep me grounded, motivated, and remind me what matters most.

My mom—Thank you for your strength, for always believing in me, and for loving the stories before they ever became a book.

Stuart and Johanne—Thank you for the lasting positive impact you've had in our lives, and for the endless encouragement for my stories and chapters.

John F.—Thank you for being a true best friend.

To the friends who encouraged me along the way:

Lesa P., Allison R., Yolande M., Jackie O., and Mark M.—Your support, insight, and honesty meant more than you know.

Teddy and Sarah W., Marc and Cris R., Danny and Debbie M., Bobby and Patty G.—Thank you for always showing up with warmth, generosity, and support for the vision that turned into this book.

To mentors like Stuart H., John C., Scott G., Allison R., Richard L., and Bob D.—thank you for your friendship, your time, your honesty, and the way you helped me see what was ahead.

To every teammate I've had the privilege to lead—past and present—thank you. You've challenged me, taught me, and sharpened my thinking. I carry those lessons with me always.

Mike O.—For introducing me to leadership books so many years ago that shaped my thinking. You didn't just suggest them—you brought your leadership team into a journey of growth and learning that changed the way we saw everything.

Some of the authors and thinkers whose work in leadership and personal growth helped shape my perspective include:

Captain Mike Abrashoff, Brené Brown, James Clear, Carol Dweck, David Goggins, Jon Gordon, Jesse Itzler, John O'Leary, Mel Robbins, Shonda Rhimes, Arnold Schwarzenegger, Simon Sinek, and Jack Welch.

Vanessa M.—the most impactful editor I could have hoped for on this book. Thank you for your clarity, speed, and care. Your guidance and flexibility made all the difference in bringing this to the finish line.

Aaron

We did it. That's the end.
I trust the journey was both
fulfilling and inspiring.

One meaningful way to help others
discover this book is to leave a review
on Amazon and/or Goodreads.

For a first-time, self-published author,
your feedback helps carry the message
further than I ever could on my own.

Thank you for being part
of something impactful.

www.ingramcontent.com/pod-product-compliance
Lightning Source LLC
Chambersburg PA
CBHW040230110526
44582CB00001B/1